The Colonial Tavern

A Glimpse of New England Town Life – a Social History of America's Bars in the 1600s and 1700s

By Edward Field

PANTIANOS
CLASSICS

Published by Pantianos Classics

ISBN-13: 978-1-78987-196-8

First published in 1897

Contents

"I'll view the manners of the town,
Peruse the traders, gaze upon the buildings.
And then return, and sleep within mine inn;"

— Comedy of Errors, Act i. Scene 2.

Preface

The material that has been used to produce these reflections from the Colonial tavern has been gleaned from many sources. The various New England town histories and newspapers have disclosed many a curious item; old diaries, letters, account books and other writings have been studiously examined and their quaint entries liberally made use of; while state, town and court records have brought to light many forgotten episodes that have gone far to make up this picture of one side of the life in New England during the seventeenth and eighteenth centuries.

The list of printed volumes which have been consulted in preparing this book includes the following admirable town histories: Roads' *"Marblehead"* Temple's *"Brookfield"* Tilden's *"Medfield"* Usher's *"Medford"* Stark's *"Dunbarton"* Smith's *"Newburyport,"* Chase's *"Haverhill"* Orcutt's *"Dorchester"* Paige's *"Cambridge"* Coffin's *"Newbury"* Forbes' *"Hundredth Town"* (Westborough), Atwater's *"New Haven Colony"* Lewis' *"Lynn and Nahant"* and Nourse's *"Lancaster."* To these volumes, and to many others, I am indebted for much that has made my story more complete.

E. F.

Providence, Rhode Island, December, 1896.

Chapter One - The Colonial Tavern

IN the early settlements in New England, the tavern, inn or ordinary as it was variously called, was second only in importance to the colonial meeting house. Their relationship too, strange as it may seem, was of the most intimate character. The tavern was usually located near the meeting house, and this in some communities was the condition under which the tavern license was granted. John Vyall of Boston, in 1651, so the record states, was granted "Libertie to keep a house of Comon entertainment if the Countie Court Consent, provided he keepe it neere the new meeting house." Nor was this condition confined to New England, for about this same time "Jean Boisdon, innkeeper, was required to establish himself on the great square of Quebec, close to the church."

A still closer relationship between the tavern and the meeting house is found in the annals of the town of Little Compton, (R. I.) for one of its meeting houses after serving the townsmen for many years as a place for the worship of God, and being the scene of many exciting contests between the two factions which alternately controlled its affairs, was finally abandoned for church purposes and became a house for the entertainment of travellers.

There were many good reasons for thus locating the tavern.

Lecture days, fast days, Sundays and on other church occasions, the people gathered from miles around to attend the service; there was the long prayer and sermon in the morning, the noon rest for refreshment, then the afternoon prayer and sermon, after which the townspeople departed on their journey homeward. In many towns during this nooning, between the services, the tavern became the resort of the worshippers. In the cold winter months, the comfortable warmth of the tavern fire and such other attractions as the tavern only could supply, were both appreciated and enjoyed.

Fires were never kindled within the colonial meeting house, it was always cold, damp and gloomy within them in the winter, and the congregation was forced to sit shivering until the final "lastly" was said. Some of the women brought with them little foot stoves, wherein live coals were deposited, affording some warmth during the early part of the service, but these little sparks became as cold as the temperature itself long before the sermon was brought to a close!"

"Meeting house so cold," wrote a Medford church-goer, "that the men struck their feet together and children gathered around their mothers' foot stoves."

In the summer time, it made an agreeable change to step from the meeting house to the tavern, and there in the shade discuss the news and gossip of the town, and incidentally the palate-pleasing beverages for which the tavern was known.

All news emanated from the tavern, the town meeting and the town council here assembled, the courts met in solemn dignity, the traveller full of news from his last stopping place was sometimes here found, and notices for the information of the townsmen were posted on the tavern door. At Medford it was voted "that their names posted on the several tavern doors shall be a sufficient notice for jurors."

The town meeting, however, was not always held within the tavern. The meeting house was the natural place for such gatherings, especially was this so in the Massachusetts colony, for her civil and religious affairs were closely identified. Sometimes the piercing, biting blasts of winter whistling through the cracks and crannies in the dilapidated old meeting house, drove the shivering townsmen to seek some warmer and more comfortable place to discuss and deliberate over the grave questions of state, and the vote "that the meeting be moved from the meeting house to the ordinary" was passed with great unanimity.

This proved to be a most popular vote in Medford, always without a dissenting voice, and the records of that town contain many entries where the winter meetings were "moved to the house of Samuel Sadey, inn keeper, by reason of the cold." No one ever complained of the tavern "by reason of the cold." As a rule it was always snug and comfortable; the great fireplace heaped high with blazing logs produced a cheerful warmth for the exterior, while the contents of the "buffet" stimulated an internal warmth that lived in the memories of the townsmen from one winter's town meeting to another. When these meetings were held at the tavern it was customary for the town officers and the members of the town council or selectmen, after the business had been disposed of, to repair to the living room of the tavern and dine at the expense of the town. Many times this was done openly, often secretly; however it was done the town paid the bill either "as an allowance over his said account," as one town ingeniously records it, or "for this dales fireing and hous room," as it is entered on the records of another. The town of Medfield (Mass.) in 1658 authorized its Selectmen "to dine at the ordinary at the town's expense," and it is said by the historian of that town, that an annual dinner at the public cost was all the compensation that selectmen of this town received for nearly two hundred years.

Now it was not long before the attractions of the tavern caused many of. the townsmen to forsake the meeting house and assemble at the ordinary on Sundays and Lecture days; the General Court of Massachusetts, therefore, in order to head off this backsliding, passed a law having for its object a more universal attendance on church occasions. This law required inn-keepers within one mile of the meeting to which they belonged, "to clear their houses of all persons able to go to meeting during the time of exercise," and thus, to use an apt phrase, the townsmen were "frozen out" of the tavern to be "frozen" in the meeting house. But after all there were church occasions when the tavern was not cleared of its patrons, and this was when the meeting house was raised. This was an event which was celebrated by a grand demonstration.

Long years of agitation had resulted in at last determining when, where and how the meeting house should be built. Great preparations were made for this ceremony, and the coming event was heralded throughout the neighboring country. Besides carpenters, masons, joiners and other craftsmen, lumber, stone, and other merchandize and building material, there was another commodity as essential to the occasion as all these, and that was rum. No meeting house could be properly raised unless its foundations were suitably anointed with this liquor. On such occasions the tavern was the centre of attraction. Fond anticipations of what was in store for them there stimulated the concourse of mechanics and helpers to their best efforts, and when at last the master workman announced that the new meeting house was duly and truly raised, then there came what was called in those days "rioting in the tavern." The records of the town of Medfield furnish a vivid illustration of what was necessary on such occasions.

The wants of that town had made the erection of a new meeting house an absolute necessity; the usual discussion and dispute as to the site, size and cost came to an end, and the actual work was commenced.

On the day appointed for the "raising" people came from miles around, teams lined the village streets, booths were erected where cakes and beer were sold, and the whole place took on a holiday appearance Besides the great army of craftsmen, crowds of men, women and children, attracted by the advertisement of the event, came to witness the great sight.

Manfully and diligently the people worked, and the meeting house was raised, but to accomplish it there was required "four barrels of beer, twenty-four gallons of West India rum, thirty gallons of New England rum, thirty-five pounds of loaf sugar, twenty-five pounds of brown sugar, and four hundred and sixty-five lemons." It was a busy day, too, at the taverns, for the two inn-keepers in the town furnished, on this occasion, besides the liquors mentioned, "seven hundred and fifteen meals for the men that assisted at the raising at 6d a meal." All this expense for meals, rum, beer, sugar and lemons was paid out of the town treasury by direct vote of the freemen. This was a most common custom, and the records of New England are full of such illustrations. Sometimes special licenses were given to tavern keepers on such occasions, as in Salem in 1673, when Nathaniel Ingerson was "allowed to sell bear and syder by the quart for the tyme whyle the farmers are a building of their meeting house," but it is somewhat surprising to learn that in these good old days, when such rigorous laws regulated the conduct of the people on Sundays and other church days, when walking on the streets and such trivial pastimes were forbidden, that with this privilege there was added the further liberty of selling beer and cider "on Lord's days thereafter." Sunday selling was actually licensed in Salem town in 1673, while to-day special officers watch the express and freight offices that no liquors be brought within the precincts of the town. [1]

The early' settlers in New England were considerably disturbed owing to their inability to obtain liquors. Beer was the common drink in Old England, and the emigrants to New England eagerly looked forward to the time when it would be possible to obtain the beverage of the mother country. Water they did drink from necessity, but with great reluctance, notwithstanding its purity in contrast with that which they had obtained at home.

Thomas Dudley, writing in 1630, regarding the settlement of the Bay Colony, advises those who contemplate establishing themselves in the new world that there may be found, among other things, "good water to drink," and then adds, doubtless to cheer any despondency of feelings that might result from the suggestion of water, "till wine or beer can be made."

They were not long, however, in providing themselves with this latter article, for a brew house was considered just as essential to a homestead as the barn or crib, and in the New Haven colony, it is said, "beer was on the table as regularly as bread."

In 1662 the elders of the New Haven church seemed likely to lose their supply of beer, and this alarming situation was considered of sufficient moment to be laid before the town authorities, and "Deacon Park informed the town that they were much troubled to supply the elders with wheat and malt, and he feared there was want, therefore desired the town to consider of it." Due consideration was given this complaint and it was recorded, "the deputy governor urged it that men would endeavor to make a present supply for them." Why the elders were brought to such straits does not appear. Perhaps it may have been caused by the demands of church occasions.

There was a privilege which the tavern enjoyed that could not be found elsewhere — this was the right to sell liquors. In early colonial days the habit of drinking liquor was indulged in by all classes, men, women and children. It was a habit brought to New England from the mother country, and to gratify this desire for alcoholic stimulants the tavern early became a public necessity.

The extent to which this habit was carried caused the authorities soon to recognize the importance of regulating the sale of liquors. That this traffic might not be carried on surreptitiously in the sparsely settled communities, where there was no great necessity for a public house, the General Court of Massachusetts, in 1656, had by legislative enactment made the towns liable to a fine for not sustaining an ordinary, and in some cases this fine was imposed and collected time after time for disregarding the law.

In 1682, Hugh March of Newbury, who had presided over the destinies of the only tavern in that town for a period of twelve years, petitioned the county court for a renewal of his license. In this petition he says: "The town of Newbury some years since were destitute of an ordinary and could not persuade any person to keep it. For want of an ordinary they were twice fined by the county, and would have been a third time had I not undertaken it. It cost me one hundred and twenty pounds to repair the house and more than four hundred pounds in building house, barn, stable, and so forth." Such a public benefactor certainly was entitled to the greatest consideration, and his license soon followed his petition. The town of Concord (Mass.) found itself in a similar predicament in 1660, and for not having a common house of entertainment was "presented" by the grand jury, and for this neglect was fined 2s and 6d; besides this the town was admonished "to have a meet person" nominated at the next court for such a purpose or it would be subject to a penalty of £5. Newburyport established its tavern in 1656, and thereby just escaped the fine which other towns were called upon to pay. In 1668 there was no tavern in the town of Newbury, and of course no licensed place for the sale of liquors. But that was not the worst of it, for there was no one within the town's boundaries who appeared desirous of conducting one. This was a condition to which the townsmen could not quite reconcile themselves. If they could not get a tavern they must have a place where they could obtain liquor, there was a substantial meeting house, a goodly number of worshippers, and doubtless believing

> "There's naught no doubt so much
>   the spirit cheers,
> As rum and true religion."

The townsmen prevailed upon one of their number to undertake the sale of liquor on high moral grounds, and in that year the selectmen and the principal inhabitants petitioned the court at Salem that "Captain Paul White be licensed to sell wine out of doors by retail for the necessary relief of some sick or other indigent persons by whom the churches exegencies have sundry times been supplied, who also may the more conveniently accommodate the churches occasions from time to time until some man be licensed to keep ordinary here."

The business which Captain White was thus forced into, eventually got him into trouble. He found the occupation both profitable and agreeable, and in addition to church occasions he seems to have sold liquor on all occasions, continuing to do so until 1673, when Hugh March, who had come to the aid of the town three years before, and had established himself as the regularly licensed innkeeper, complained to the county court against his neighbor White for selling wine; alleging in his bill of complaint, "so it is that Captain White under colour of providing the sacrament wine, doth frequently retaile wines unto the inhabitants and others to the damage and disabling your petitioner."

As the settlements in New England became more populous, the demand for public houses for the accommodation of travellers journeying from one part of the country to another became more necessary; and thus it came about that the town of Brookfield in 1691 had its wants in this respect supplied, the General Court finding that "ye continuall passing of travellers to & from ye

Bay through Brookfield doth in good sobrietie bespeake for a retailer of strong drink to be allowed to yt place; "a license was granted to Samuel Owen "to sell drinke provided he take serious care to keepe good rule & order in all his soe selling." Maintaining good rule and order was one of the conditions under which all tavern licenses were granted. There were others, for "such games as are judged by the Laws of England to be unlawfull in such Comon houses as Carding, Dicing, Slide Groat, &c.," were prohibited, as was also the games of "Shuffel board," quoits, loggets, bowls, nine -pins and billiards. The form of license varied in the different Colonies and Counties, some were brief containing only a few lines, while others were full and explicit.

The license granted to Eleazer Arnold of Providence (R. I.) by the town council was in the following words:

"Whereas the Lawes do Provide that no Person Inhabiting in our Collony shall Keepe any Publick house of Entertainment for strangers Travilers or others, nor Retale strong drinke, unless they have a license from the Council of ye Respective Towne whereunto they do belong; And whereas you justice Eleazer Arnold Inhabitant of this Towne of Providence in ye Cdlloney of Rhode Island & Providence Plantations in New England haveing desired of ye Towne Councill of sd Providence that they would grant unto you a licence in order to that Purpose, whereby you might be in a Capacitye to Keepe a house of that Order, & for that imploy: The Town Council of said Providence being mett & haveing Considered your request and to ye End that Strangers Travilers & other Persons may be accommodated with suteable Entertainment at all times as Ocation Requires do by these presents Grant unto you ye abovesd Justice Eleazer Arnold licence & libertye to Keepe a Publick house of Entertainment in sd Providence Towneshipp, at your dwelling for the entertaineing of Strangers Travilers & other Persons, both horse & foote Carters Drovers &c at all times for & duiring the full & just terme of one yeares Time forward from ye day of ye date of these presentes, And that at all times duiring, the said terme of Time you do (within your Prescinckes) well & truly observe do & Keepe good Orders according as ye lawes do Require persons who are licensed to Keepe such houses to do & Performe. Dated August ye 14th 1710."

The first tavern keeper in Medford was granted a license in the following words:

"Nathaniel Pierce of Medford is permitted to sell liquors unto such sober minded neighbors as he shall think meet, so as he sell not less than the quantity of a gallon at a time to one person and not in smaller quantities by retail to the occasioning of drunkenness."

The license to Mary Pray of Providence contained the injunction not "to suffer any unlawful game to be used in yr house nor any Evill Rule to be kept therein but doe behave yourself according to ye Lawes Established." Laws were enacted regulating the conduct of such places after license had issued.

Col. Thomas Howe kept a tavern in Marlborough in 1696, and the bond which he gave to the County Court for the proper conduct of his house contained these provisions: "He shall not suffer or have any playing at cards, dice, tally, bowls, nine pins, billiards, or any other unlawful game or games in his said house, or yard, or gardens, or backside, nor shall he suffer to remain in his house any person or persons, not being his own family, on Saturday night after dark, or on the Sabbath days, or during the time of Gods Public Worship; nor shall he entertain as lodgers in his house any strangers men or women, above the space of forty-eight hours, but such whose names and surnames he shall deliver to one of the selectmen or constables of the town, unless they shall be such as he very well knoweth, and will ensure for his or their forthcoming — nor shall sell any wine to the Indians or negroes, nor suffer any children or servant, or other person to remain in his house, tippling or drinking after nine o'clock in the night — nor shall buy or take to preserve any stolen goods, nor willingly or knowingly harbor in his house, barn, stable, or otherwhere any rougues, vagabonds, thieves, sturdy beggars, masterless men and women, or other notorious offenders whatsoever — nor shall any person or persons whatsoever, sell or utter any wine, beer, ale, cider, rum, brandy, or other liquors by defaulting or by color of his license — nor shall entertain any person or persons to whom he shall be prohibited by law, or by any one of the magistrates of the county as persons of jolly conversation or given to tippling."

Thus did Puritan Massachusetts frown on jollity, and it was "so nominated in the bond."

Notwithstanding the restrictions of the law, unlawful games were indulged in by the people. In the dull life which must have characterized their existence, it would seem strange if their exuberant spirits did not sometimes overcome their respect for the law and cause them to engage in a friendly game of nine pins, but it did not stop there, for we have more or less positive evidence that they desecrated the Lord's Day by taking part in the game. Othniel Gorton kept tavern at Mashantatuck, near Providence, and it seems that such irregular proceedings took place at his house as well as at one of his neighbors, which brought forth the following complaint to one of the Magistrates, Major Thomas Fenner. "The complaint of moses bartlet to maigor fenner, friend, i am creadibly informed by Samuel Westcot: that last first day of the week (it being the Sabbath) which was the 12 day of this month called July said Westcot said he was at Othniel gortons and with him Edward Potter and James Briggs and they saw him said Gorton seling strong drink and entertaining people playing nine pins and further the abovesaid persons were at Thomas Burlingame juniors the above said day and saw their the like disorderly wicked doings July 19, 1713.   Moses bartlet.

P. S. My friend pray consider that when in our town any man in conscience towards god cannot actively submit to some law he is dealt with to the full extent but some that sin against their conscience and it appears are carefully handled."

12

In Massachusetts drunkenness or tippling was prohibited, and the tavern keeper who permitted such irregularities was liable to a fine of ten shillings. Excessive drinking about a tavern was visited with a fine of thirty shillings and two pence, and lest there might be some doubt in the minds of the over-indulgent townsmen, excessive drinking was defined to be "when above half a pint of wine is allowed at one time to one person."

Tavern keepers were also restricted in their charges to patrons, "vj d a meal," and not above "j d for an ale quart of beare out of meale tyme."

Associated with the mugs of beer, the roaring fire, and the stories and gossip of the tap room, is the solace of a pipe of tobacco, but this latter comfort was denied habitues of the tavern for the landlords were forbidden "to suffer any tobacco to be taken into their houses under the penalty of vs for evry offence, to be payde by the victualer, and xij d by the party that takes it." But the law relating to the use of tobacco did not stop there, the private use was regulated and restricted, for it was provided "that noe person shall take tobacco publiquely, under the penalty of ij s vj d, nor privately, in his own house, or in the house of another, before strangers, and that two or more shall not take it together any where, under the aforesaid penalty for evry offence." The law-making authority of the Massachusetts Bay Colony was continually adopting measures looking toward a more temperate use of liquors. A penalty of five pounds was imposed on the innkeeper if any person "shall be made drunke" in his house or any immoderate drinking suffered, and he was even liable to the forfeiture of his license and the loss of his sign, an important adjunct to the institution. Notwithstanding the excessive use of liquors in colonial days, drunkenness was not tolerated, and over-indulgence in stimulants was visited with heavy penalties; fines were imposed on such offenders, and they were required to sit in the stocks with a card upon their breasts, on which the letter D was conspicuously displayed. The records of the colonial courts are full of cases where punishments were inflicted for breaches of the law with respect to the use of liquors.

At Boston, "the 16th of the 12th mo, 1642, William Willoughby for being distempered with wine and mispending his time and neglecting both publique and private Ordinances was commited to Prison to be kept to worke there." Robert Wright a year later was "fined twenty shillings for being twice distempered in drink or to sit an hour in the stocks the next Market day at Boston." These punishments, however, were not entirely directed against the unfortunate person whose will was controlled by his appetite.

The person who supplied him was likewise subjected to punishment, and for a breach of the condition of his license, and for disregarding the provisions of the law, the County Court in 1632 caused the liquors belonging to a Dorchester man to be forfeited, by ordering that "the remaind' of Mr Aliens stronge water being estimated about 2 gallands shalbe delivered into the hands of the deacons of Dorchester for the benefit of the poor there, for his sellinge of it dyvrs tymes to such as were drunke with it, hee knowing thereof."

It would be interesting to know in what manner the good deacons of Dorchester applied this two gallons of strong water for the benefit of the poor. Another indiscreet tavern keeper was Nicholas Rogers, and in 1643, "for his drunkenness and making others drunke with his strong waters was censured to be whipped."

As early as 1637 complaints had been made "that much drunkenness waste of the good creatures of God mispense of precious time and other disorders" had occurred at the Taverns, and additional legislation was forthwith enacted to remedy, if possible, this evil. A complete prohibition was not considered desirable, so the ingenious remedy was suggested of reducing the quality of the brews and thereby reduce the liability of "much drunkenness and waste of the good creatures of God." So the General Court passed a law which provided that "it shall not be lawfull for any persons that shall keepe any inn or common victualing house to sell or have in their houses any wine, nor strong waters nor any beare or other drink other than such as may and shall be sould for id the quart at the most," and that no beer should be brewed by an inn holder or victualler, but only by licensed brewers. Such persons, however, should "not sell or utter any beare or other drinke of any stronger size than such as may and shall be afforded at the rate of 8shs the barrell." But it was no use, the liquor traffic was as difficult to compass then as it is now, and the next year inn holders and victuallers were permitted to brew their own beer, and a few years later the restraint as to selling beer at "1d the quart" was repealed.

The tavern was the common gathering place for the whole community, and its doors were open to all comers with the exception of apprentices, negroes and Indians. Every indenture of apprentice, girl or boy, contained this clause: "Taverns nor Ale houses he shall not frequent Except it be about his said master or mistress their business," and it is fair to assume that this direction was heeded.

There was in all the colonies a law prohibiting the sale of liquors to Indians, but unlike the previous prohibition, it is safe to say that this was universally disregarded. In Providence the law "that restraineth men from selling wine or Liquors to ye Indians" was repealed in 1656, whether to prevent moral corruption or to make business at the taverns more profitable, there is no way of ascertaining from the records. In the town of Haverhill the sale of liquors to those "devilish salvages" was visited with a heavy penalty, and in 1683 John Page of that town was fined "forty shillings for selling drink to the Indians."

Haverhill men had no love for the red heathen, or for any one who catered to their wants, for theirs had been a hard struggle against the ravages of these creatures from the very earliest days of the settlement of the town, and it was destined to be so for nearly a century. Ayer's Tavern at Brookfield was the scene of one of the most desperate encounters with the Indians during King Philip's war. Some of the old tavern keepers were on the most friendly terms with the red men. Major Thomas Fenner, who kept a tavern in the

14

town of Providence, almost under the shadows of the boulder-capped hill of Neutaconconit, employed them about his farm, sheltered them within his house, and in his capacity as Justice protected them from being wronged by their white neighbors, while Eleazer Arnold, whose license has been previously mentioned, had among his effects when he died "an old bed the Indians used to Lie on" listed in the inventory of his estate. Previous to the beginning of the eighteenth century the tavern was no such institution as it afterwards became There were few travelers passing from town to town who were forced to find accommodations at the public house, and its uses and purposes were mainly for drinking, the interchange of news and opinions, and its incidental sociability.

In the seaport towns like Salem, Marblehead, Boston, Newport, Providence, and the settlements along the Connecticut shore, there was a greater necessity for them, for the fisheries early attracted large numbers of hardy New Englanders, and trading vessels frequently sailed into the ports to barter all sorts of commodities for furs and products of the soil.

A glimpse inside one of these ancient hostelries is convincing proof that there was little for the comfort of the traveler save in one respect, and that was the paraphernalia of the tap room. That was sufficient, however, to provide for most any demand that might have been made. In 1674 John Whipple of Providence, who had come to that town from "good old Dorchester," was granted a license to "keepe a house of Intertainment." During the years that he catered to the wants of man and beast this was a famous place of resort. In 1685 death visited the Whipple tavern, and called to his long home the aged tavern keeper. His estate, in due course of time, was administered, and the inventory of his property spread upon the records. From this it appears that his house consisted of but two rooms, "ye lower room" and "ye chamber." Doubtless there was a "lean too," for most of the early houses had this addition to its structure, being used for all sorts of purposes. In the "lower room" there was "an old bed stead and a bed cord" "a cubbard press" "3 old curtains & a valian" (vallance) "an old Rotten feather bed about 12 pounds of old feathers in it" "a joynt work chest I joyner worke chair" and "3 other chairs." In the chamber were "two feather beds and bolster (one old)" "a whitish cotton rug an old torne sheet a part of a bed stud and bed cord" "i pillow and pillow case" a "Red Coverlidd a bed blanket, much worne, three sheets" "three broken joynt stools and a Court Cubbard."

Surely this was not what one would expect to find in a house for the entertainment of travelers who were forced to abide for a night or so, — one bedstead, three feather beds, one of little use, and a chest, for

"The chest contrived a double debt to pay,
  A bed by night a chest of drawers by day."

The weary traveler could not have found great comfort in a night's lodging with mine host Whipple. But the early taverns were not contrived nor intended for such guests. They were equipped for those who came in during the day for a mug of ale or some such beverage, or in the evening up to nine o'clock, when the law required the tavern door should be closed.

The articles at Whipple's tavern for the use of such guests were not wanting, however, for this old inventory tells us there were pewter basins, quart pots, pint pots, gill pots, a Tankard pint pot, "beere boules," spoons, glass bottles and other dishes, and these were more in demand than the "old fether beds," broken "bedstuds" and "old Red Coverlidd."

In the larger towns, taverns were more pretentious and commodious, greater attention was paid to the paraphernalia of the tap-room, and better accommodations in this respect were afforded patrons, but in all, the facilities for the dispensing of liquors was the conspicuous feature of the house. In contrast with Whipple's tavern was the "King's Arms" at Boston, which formerly stood in what is now called Dock Square, and kept by one Hugh Gunnison. After nine years of business at this house, Gunnison sold out in 1651 to Henry Shrimpton for the sum of £600 sterling. Every room in this house bore some distinguishing name, like the inns in Old England, there was the "Exchange," the "Court Chamber," where it is said the General Court of the Colony dined on certain occasions, the "London" and "Star." One piece of furniture contained in the "Exchange" chamber was "one half headed bedstead with blew pillars," a most elaborate piece of furniture evidently. These rooms were on the upper floor of the house and were for the use of the "quality" of the town who desired to take their refreshments privately. Below was the "hall," the great common room, which contained three stalls "with a bar convenient to it;" this was the public drinking place.

Another Boston tavern was the "Blue Anchor," and its rooms were distinguished by such names as the "Cross Keys," "Green Dragon," "Anchor and Castle Chamber," and the "Rose and Sun Low Room."

There were other places perhaps as elaborately apportioned as these, but the majority of the public houses in Boston at this period were not unlike the Whipple establishment, for a few years later Cotton Mather said that every other house in Boston was an ale house. The complaint of the scarcity of taverns did not last long, the cause was removed, for like a rank weed they increased and multiplied, at last becoming so numerous that the General Court of Massachusetts was obliged to delegate the authority to license them to the county courts, that it might not be "thereby hindered in their more weighty affairs" of state. Soon complaints began to be made that taverns were too numerous and their influence was demoralizing the whole of New England. The important position which the tavern keeper held in the community incited others to enter into a similar occupation. Intrigue, political scheming, and influence of all kinds and character was brought to bear upon the lawmaking authorities and licenses were granted without limit, the old laws which provided that only "godly persons '" and "meet persons" receive licenses was lost sight of, and the person who had a "pull" at court got his license irrespective of his character or the reputation of his place.

Nathaniel Saltonstall of Haverhill, "a man of superior powers of mind and rare talents," was one of the earliest men of prominence to boldly denounce the tavern. He was one of the Assistants, an officer in the militia, and on account of his great learning was appointed one of the judges in the Salem witchcraft trials, but being a man of learning he refused to serve, a fact which shows that he was a man of ideas far in advance of his times. His letter which follows, written on a sick bed, and sent to the Salem Court, gives a vivid idea of the perniciousness of the public houses, and is a strong protest against them. It was written on the 26th day of December, 1696.

Much Hond. Gentlemen:

I allways thought it great prudence and Christianity in our former leaders and rulers, by their laws to state the number of publique houses in towns and for regulation of such houses, as were of necessity, thereby to pi-event all sorts, almost, of wickedness which daily grow in upon us like a flood. But alas, I see not but that now, the care is over, and such (as to some places I may term them) pest houses and' places of enticement, (tho not so intended by the Justices) to sin are multiplied. It is multiplied too openly, that the cause of it may be, the price of retailers fees &c. I pray what need of six retailers in Salisbury and of more than one in Haverhill, and some other towns, where the people, when taxes and rates for the country and ministers are collecting, with open mouths complain of povertie and being hardly dealt with, and yet I am fully informed, can spend much time, and spend their estate at such blind holes, as are clandestinely and unjustly petitioned for, and more threaten to get licenses, chiefly by repairing to a remote court, where they are not known or suspected, but pass for current, and thereby the towns are abused and the youth get evil habits, and men sent out on country service, at such places waste much of their time, yet expect pay for it, in most pernicious loytering and what, and sometimes by foolish if not potvaliant firing and shooting off guns, not for the destruction of enemies, but to the wonderful disturbance and affrightment of the inhabitants, which is not the service, a scout is allowed and maintained for. Please to see if possible, what good is done by giving a license to Robert Hastings, in such a by place about three miles from the publique house in town. The man himself I am sure has no cause, nor do I believe the town or travellers if they are sober men, will ever give the court thanks for the first grant to him, or the further renewal thereof.

But now the bravado is made, what is done is not enough, we must have a third tippling house at Peter Patey's about midway between the other two, which they boast as cocksure of, and have it is thought laid in, for this very end, an unaccountable store of cyder, rum molasses and what not. It is well if this stock be not now spent on, in procure subscriptions for to obtain the villain's license, which I fear, knowing the man, we may be bold to say, wickedness will be practised and without control, and we must be quiet, or hated because of licenses for something which they will enlarge to any and every-thing which is not &c * * *

It would be good, if the law or rule of Court made, were duly practiced as to granting and renewing of licenses, that none be meddled with but at the court to which the grand jurors do repair, belonging to the town where the man lives who petition for license, so that the court may see what complaints are entered by bill, or better inquiries may be made. But now many that would speak if they had knowledge of the motion before the grant was made, cannot. I have done my part in court, as to what I heard of, to prevent such confiding licences to persons unknown.

We need but one place to be granted for strangers, or else it were more than enough. As for the two last mentioned, none that knew the men or the places, or the business, of necessity there let be done, can judge them to con-duce to good or accommodation of civilized men. * * *

I am now God's prisoner and can't come abroad. I have waited long to speak of those and others but as yet can't meet with an opportunity. You have nothing here of personal animosity of mine against any man, but zeal and faithfulness to my country and town, and to the young and rising genera-tion that they be not too much at libertie to live and do as they list. I pray ac-cept of the good intentions of gentlemen your humble servant

N. Saltonstall.

To the Justices in Quarter Sessions setting at Salem. December 1696"

The picture drawn by Saltonstall illustrates the condition of the tavern generally throughout the New England colonies. Like everything else there were exceptions in taverns, but those that had a good name and were noted for their excellence and hospitality had to suffer on account of those that were a menace to the communities in which they were located.

The general reputation of the tavern had not changed much twenty-five years later, if the entry which Judge Sewall made in his diary can be consid-ered as evidence, for on September 20, 1721, he wrote, "Thomas Hale was made a justice. I opposed it, because there are five in Newbury already, and he had lately kept an ordinary and sold rum."

Long years after this, John Adams, who detested the public house and ex-erted all his energies to bring about a reform in their conduct, wrote that he was "Grieved to the heart to see the number of idlers, thieves, sots and con-sumptive patients made for the use of physicians, in those infamous seminar-ies. I applied to the Court of Sessions, procured a committee of inspection and inquiry, reduced the number of licensed houses, etc. But I only acquired the reputation of a hypocrite and an ambitious demagogue by it. The number of licensed houses were soon reinstated, drams, grog and sotting were not diminished, and remain to this day as deplorable as ever. You may as well preach to the Indian against rum as our people."

In contradistinction to the observations of these gentlemen on the condi-tion of the public house, we have the testimony of the Rev. Dr. Dwight, who says of the taverns in the early part of the present century, "The best old-fashioned New England inns were superior to any of the modern ones. There was less bustle, less parade, less appearance of doing a great deal to gratify your wishes than at the reputable modern inn; but much more was actually done, and there was much more comfort and enjoyment. In a word, you found in these inns the pleasures of an excellent private house. If you were sick you were nursed and befriended as in your own family. To finish the story, your bills were always equitable, calculated on what you ought to pay, and not upon the scheme of getting the most which extortion might think proper to demand." Of the appearance or condition of the tap-room this eminent divine seems to have been an uninterested or unwilling observer.

No less a personage than Dr. Johnson once said, "there is no place at which people can enjoy themselves so well as at a capital tavern like this," he was speaking of the Old Chapel House inn in Oxfordshire, "Let there be ever so great a plenty of good things, ever so much grandeur, ever so much elegance, ever so much desire that every guest should be easy; in the nature of things it cannot be. There must always be some degree of care and anxiety. The master of the house is anxious to entertain his friends; they in turn are anxious to be agreeable to him, and no one but a very impudent boy can as freely command what is in another man's house as if he were in his own. Whereas at a tavern there is a general freedom from anxiety. You are sure, you are welcome and the more noise you make, the more trouble you give, the more good things you call for, the welcomer you are. No servants will attend you with the alacrity which waiters do, who are incited by the prospect of an immediate reward in proportion as they please. No, sir; there is nothing which has yet been contrived by man by which so much happiness is produced as by a good tavern or inn."

[1] The summer of 1896.

Chapter Two - The Tavern Keeper

THERE is no more picturesque character in early Colonial life than the individual who presided over the tavern. He was a prominent personage in the management of the town affairs, was thoroughly informed on all public matters — and private matters as well; he enjoyed the confidence of all who gathered around his fireside, and, he always held public office. Indeed, to hold public office was the prerogative of the tavern keeper. His house was the rendezvous for all the townspeople, and all matters of news sooner or later, generally i sooner, were discussed around his blazing fire in winter or where the breezes blew the coolest about his place in summer. Public questions, trade, theology, science, crops, politics, scandal, local gossip and dissection of private character, were all mixed together and washed down with flip, toddy, punch and other seductive drinks of Colonial day.

The tavern keeper is differently pictured — generally good-natured, fat, obliging, good-looking and well-dressed, and well fitted for every position in which he was sooner or later called upon to play his part. He led the singing in the meeting house on Sunday; ran the ferry if his tavern was situated beside a stream; acted as schoolmaster for the children of those who frequented his house; served his fellow men in the legislature, town council, selectmen, and other minor offices; ruled with solemn dignity over the local courts; headed the — Train Band on training or squadron days; kept order in the meeting house on Sundays; surveyed the lands assigned to the land-crazy townsmen; had met with all sorts of adventures, which he delighted in telling and re-telling; and in fact, next to the town clerk, was the most important and learned man in the place.

Some were frugal and thrifty and acquired great wealth, some penurious and mean, while others were extravagant and wasted their estate and at last were forced to spend their declining years in poverty and be classed among the town's poor. It has been said that "some landlords were so full of sunshine that it was June all the year round; others had minds so frost-bitten that there was no hope for you except in the January thaw. Here was one so anxious to oblige that he would spring to throw a lassoo around the moon if you wished it, and then another so cross that putting a question to him was like squeezing a lemon." As a rule, however, the landlord of the tavern was a man whose company was sought for its cheer and comfort. Contact with people had brought him much experience and had sharpened his wits, and it was a smart man who got the best of him in an argument, trade, or a joke. A Medford tavern keeper being accused by one of his customers with watering his liquors too freely, quietly remarked, "More water, more conscience," turned on his heels and walked away.

A Connecticut tavern keeper who attempted to indulge in a bit of fun with an untutored child of the forest, had the tables turned upon him. "Along in the fall of the year an Indian came to his house for a dram, which the tavern keeper supplied and for which he charged him twopence. The next spring the Indian again appeared, ordered his drink, and was somewhat surprised to be charged threepence. 'How is this, landlord!' says he, 'last fall you asked but two coppers for a glass of rum, now you ask three.' 'Oh,' says the landlord, 'it costs me a good deal to keep rum over winter; it is as expensive to keep rum over winter as a horse!' 'My,' says the Indian, 'I can't see through that; he won't eat so much hay, — *maybe he drink as much water!*'"

The ingenuity which they practiced to evade laws or to make more popular their houses is shown in the conduct of mine host Coffin of Newbury. In 1653 the Newbury tavern was presided over by Tristam Coffin and his good wife Dionis. At that time there was a law in force in Massachusetts which provided that "Every person licensed to keep an ordinary shall always be provided with good wholesome beere of four bushels of malt to the hogshead, which he shall not sell above two pence the ale quart on penalty of forty shillings the first offence and for the second offence shall lose his license."

Coffin and his wife doubtless in the privacy of the domestic circle discussed this law and tried to devise some plan by which a greater popularity could be given to the attractions of their house than was afforded at their neighbors, and yet not make themselves liable for any infraction of the law.

This "four gallons of malt to the hogshead" as the standard of strength of beer was not productive of an over attractive concoction at "two pence the quart," but how to get around it was a question. In the dull light of closing day Dame Coffin sat thinking over this problem, when suddenly she arose, went to the shelf by the side of the fireplace and took down her "Hodder's Arithmetic," the household text book on this branch of learning at this period. She turned the pages until her eyes at last rested upon certain rules of proportion therein, and after diligently studying the rules there laid down said, as she closed the book, "as four is to two so is six to three." "I'll have better beer than my neighbors and be paid for it. A fig for the law." It was not a great while before the Coffin tavern, notwithstanding its grewsome name, became the most popular place of resort in the town, and the extent of its popularity soon attracted the attention of the law officer of Newbury. One day he came in and caught Mrs. Coffin in the act of selling beer at three pence per quart, and straightway brought her before the authorities for this breach of the law. Nothing daunted, she appeared and defended the charge against her, and the hearing proceeded. In her own defence she offered but one witness, and "upon the testimony of Samuel Moores that she put six bushels of malt into the hogshead" she was discharged, and doubtless returned to the tavern to dispose of the rest of the brew at the same price.

Hugh Sherratt of Haverhill, who kept a tavern in that town in 1670, was a man of misfortune. He was as, popular as he was obliging, and his house was always filled with a good-natured, jolly crowd, enjoying his hospitality and good cheer. He ought to have amassed a fortune from his business and popularity, but no matter how good a trade he commanded or how diligently he worked, the proceeds of his toil vanished from his coffers like dew before the sun, money slipped through his fingers like water through a sieve, and the records of the county court are full of cases where his name appears as defendant in actions for debt.

In 1677, then in his ninety-ninth year, his property having all been taken from him on account of this failing, poor, aged, broken down Sherratt, was forced to abandon his home and throw himself upon the mercy of the town for his support. The town authorities promptly "agreed with Peter Brewer to keep him for five shillings per week," during the short time that he had to live.

Half of this compensation was to be paid in breadstuffs and the other half in meat, and Sherratt's fellow townsmen remembering, no doubt, the many hours of enjoyment at the ordinary with this venerable and good-natured man, generously responded, and there is recorded on the records of this ancient town the names of his fellow townsmen, and the quantities of meat, pork, corn, wheat, "turnops," and other provisions which they subscribed for their old friend's support. 'Tis a sad, pathetic tale these stained and yellow pages tell, a story unusual in the annals of the tavern.

This year seems to have been an unfortunate one for Haverhill landlords, for Daniel Ela, another tavern keeper, awoke one morning to find that "the smallpox had broken out in his family," and business at his place consequently came to a standstill. During the prevalence of this distemper the time for which his license had been granted expired, and when returning health permitted him to again open his doors to the public, there was everything in shape save the necessary authority to dispose of his stock-in-trade; he therefore went before the court with a petition, alleging that on account of this episode in his family history he was unable to sell his liquors within the time covered by his license, and the court generously extended it. Small-pox about a tavern was about as serious a happening as could befall it, yet it seemed necessary for the town council of Providence to pass a law forbidding tavern keepers to harbor small-pox patients; they seem to have been permitted to harbor most anybody else, but the town wisely declared that the line must be drawn somewhere, and small-pox patients were forced to accommodate themselves elsewhere. Providence tavern keepers must have been a curious lot to make necessary the adoption of such an order.

In some cases the men who presided over the ordinaries in New England had followed a similar occupation in old England, where it was recognized as an "honest collinge," and where a long apprenticeship was necessary to perfect a person in the art and mystery of this trade or profession. Armitage's tavern in Lynn was the most celebrated caravansary in that section of the Massachusetts Bay Colony, and it continued to be for a hundred and seventy years. In 1630 Joseph Armitage, a tailor, established himself here, and as the location of the tavern was just half way between Salem and Boston, it was a favorite stop for the dignitaries of the Colony, Court officers and all persons having business before the Courts of Essex County in Salem town. The house was called the "Anchor." Notwithstanding the fact that Armitage had a good business, he, too, like poor Sherratt of Haverhill, was continually involved in pecuniary difficulties. Not satisfied with the respectable income from his tavern, he embarked in certain speculations which finally ruined him and affected his title to and authority over the house, and in June, 1643, my wife, Jane Armitage, presented her petition to the General Court praying that it would "reconfirm the custody of the said ordinary to the petitioner" and her husband. As showing the estimation in which Goodman Armitage was held by his townsmen, "two ministers and thirty-two other principal inhabitants" of Lynn endorsed this petition, all of which, no doubt, influenced the court to grant the request, for on the 26th of October it was ordered that "Joseph Armitage is allowed to keep the ordinary, but not to draw wine." This latter privilege was either later restored to him by competent authority, or he restored it himself on his own authority, for he was selling "beare & wyne" to some of the most influential and important dignitaries in the Colony. Governor Endicott and his attendants stopped there in "going to the election" in

1651, and had "vitalls bear and logen." Simon Bradstreet made it his regular stop for years. Prisoners in the custody of the law officers of the colony were here put up over night while on their journey to the lockup, and the bills of charges for all these entertainments at the Armitage Anchor are yet preserved.

Governor Endicott cannot be charged with extravagance in his official peregrinations, even though cruel persecutions are laid up against this hard hearted Puritan, for from Armitage's bill it appears "The governers Expenses from the Court of election 1651 till the end of October 1651" were:

"to beare and cacks	6d
beare & cacks to himself and some other gentlemen is	1s 2d
beare & cacks with Mr. Downing	1s 6d
beare & a cack	6d
	⎯⎯
	3s 8d"

The picture of Governor Endicott sitting at table in the "Anchor" eating "cacks" and drinking "beare" robs this picturesque character in Colonial history of some of its lustre. The lesser lights in official circles run up a bill during the same period of a much greater amount.

"bear and cacks		1s	2d
for vitalls beare and logen			5s
to Benjamin Scarlet the Governors man			8d
bear & vittells	2s		
to the Sargents		1s	9d
beear & cacks		1s	
to a man that Carried a letter to warne a Court about the dutchmen		1s	6d
to the Sargeants		1s	2d
		⎯⎯	⎯⎯
		14s	3d"

These bills were directed paid by the following order:

"Mr Auditer I pray you give a note to Mr Treasurer for the payment of 17s 11d according to these two bills of Joseph Armitage. Date the 7th of the 11th mo 1651.

Jo Endicott."

Simon Bradstreet, so long in the service of the Bay colony, was not extravagant in his wants when official duties brought him to the hospitable door of Armitage's tavern. His score reads, "due to goodman Armitage for beare and wyne att severall times as I came by in the space of aboute 3 years 4s 3d May 15 '49 more for my man & horse as hee returned home the last year when I was a Commissioner hee being detayned a sabbath day 6s 8d"

Simon Bradstreet"

One trip of his "man & horse" cost considerably more than Bradstreet's three year's expenses, but perhaps the "man & horse" had "cacks," which Bradstreet seems to have omitted from his bill of fare.

But it was the constables having prisoners in charge who made the tavern bills run up, and brings to mind the wail of Nathaniel Saltonstall when he complained so bitterly of the action "of the men sent out on country service," who "at such places waste much of their time;" though he wrote many years later, time had not improved the conduct of those in the public service, as the bill against the Colony for entertainment at the Anchor, and paid by order of the Magistrates, plainly shows:

> " To Henry Skerry with A. Udall
> a prisoner   3s 10d
> To John Keching with Abner
> Ardway to the prison   3s
> To the constable when Rubin
> went to prison   3s 10d
> To them that carried Robert
> Hatheway to prison from
> Salesbery   4s 10d
> _____
> 15s 6d"

It is doubtful if these curious illustrations of tavern life and gubernatorial junkets would have been preserved to recall such habits and customs of colonial times if they had been promptly paid. But it was not until some time after Armitage had given up the duties of tavern keeper, when being still in straightened circumstances, he presented the following complaint to the court in Salem to have these accounts adjusted.

"To the Honered Court now sitting at Salem:

The Humble pitition of Joseph Armitage, Humbly sheweth that in the time that I kept Ordinary there was some expences at my Hows by some of the Honored magistrates & Deputys of this County as apears by the bills charged oupon the Auditer Generall, which I never Receaved.

Therfor your Humbell petticionir doth humbly request this Court that they would give me an order to the County Treasurer for my pay & so your poure petitioner shall ever pray for your prosperity.

Joseph Armitage."

Following Armitage there came to the "Anchor" another individual who was in its minutest detail the ideal colonial tavern keeper, this person was Captain Thomas Marshall. He arrived in Lynn from London in the latter part of 1635, and soon after became a freeman of the colony. Lynn life at that period was not active enough for a man of his peculiar temperament, and the events which later transpired in England, when the ambitious Cromwell proceeded with his designs, gave to Marshall an opportunity of adding to his reputation and prowess as a warrior. He returned to England, joined the Cromwellian forces, and if his own statements can be relied on, sat on the right side of the Lord Protector, and was elevated to the rank of Captain, which position he filled with great honor. His restless nature again forced him back to Lynn, where he arrived with the title of Captain and full of the glory of his valiant military service. He became at once the most popular and important man in the town. Having purchased the Armitage establishment and settled down to the congenial duty of tavern keeper, he naturally ran for office, and was elected a representative to the General Court six times in succession. For more than forty years he carried on the Anchor tavern, catering to the wants of the public with great assiduity and making the tavern the most attractive of any in the town. Nothing delighted him so much as to sit down with a goodly company, which was always found about the place, and recite his experiences in the war. John Dunton, who travelled through this section of the Bay Colony in 1686, has left an account of his visit to Marshall's house, and in his diary he makes the following observations regarding this "fine old English gentleman," as he calls him. "About two of the clock I reached Capt. Marshall's house which is half way between Boston and Salem; here I staid to refresh nature with a pint of sack and a good fowl. Capt. Marshall is a hearty old gentleman, formerly one of Oliver's soldiers, upon which he very much values himself. He had all the history of the civil war at his fingers end, and if we may believe him Oliver did hardly anything that was considerable without his assistance, and If I'd have staid as long as he'd have talked he'd have spoiled my ramble at Salem."

Tavern keeping seems to have been a popular occupation for old Soldiers, a sort of soldier's "snug harbour." John Bullock and Samuel Beadle, "who lost their health in King Philips war," both kept tavern at Salem, where they doubtless told and re-told their experiences with the savages to eager and attentive ears.

Justice Eleazer Arnold kept tavern in Providence on the road to Mendon, and here he held the sessions of his court. This old house, built in 1687, is yet standing, solid and substantial as when Justice Arnold passed in and out its doors. It is framed with heavy oak timbers, and one end is built entirely of stone, terminating with a wonderfully curious pilastered stone chimney. The neighborhood about it is called Quinsnicket, which in the language of the red men meant "stone huts," for here in the clefts of the rocks the Indians made their winter homes. Justice Arnold seems to have been a particularly good friend to his red brethren, and they always found in his house a warm welcome.

He it was, it will be remembered, who had in his house, when the account of his personal belongings were listed by the appraisers in making up the inventory of his estate, the "old bed the Indians used to Lie on;" whether this is meant in the same sense as that related of William Penn and the Indians, where it is stated that he and the Indians used to retire to the house and lie and talk for hours, Penn doing the talking and the Indians the lying, there is nothing to determine.

Roxbury tavern keepers were mostly military men, says Drake, in his history of Roxbury, and this was true of other towns, and there was some method in this after all. Being Captain of the Train Band and tavern keeper, he was able to turn an honest penny by establishing his headquarters on Training day at his own house, and thus combine business and pleasure; indeed it was directly charged that sometimes. Train-band-captain -tavern-keepers ordered trainings when business was slack for the purpose of benefiting themselves. Captain Jesse Daggett of the "Ball and Pen" at Roxbury, was a train band captain, while John Johnson of the same town was "surveyor general of all ye armies," whatever that may have been; but his official position did not stop there, he was a town constable, and as such had much to do with regulating the conduct of the taverns, especially his own, and besides was a representative to the General Court of Massachusetts for fourteen years.

Another picture of the tavern keeper and his wife is drawn by John Adams, who thus describes the host and hostess of Treadwell's tavern at Ipswich. "Landlord and landlady are some of the grandest people alive, landlady is the great grand-daughter of Governor Endicott, and has all the great notions of high family that you find in Winslows, Hutchinsons, Quincys, Saltonstalls, Chandlers, Leonards, Otises, and as you might find with more propriety in the Winthrops. Yet she is cautious and modest about discovering it. She is a new light; continually canting and whining in a religious strain. The Governor was uncommonly strict and devout, eminently so in his day; and his great-great-grand-daughter hopes to keep up the honor of the family in hers and distinguish herself among her contemporaries as much. 'Terrible things sin causes,' sighs and groans the pangs of the new birth. 'The death of Christ shows above all things the heinous nature of sin! How awfully Mr Kent talks about death! how lightly and carelessly! I am sure a man of his years, who can talk so about death, must be brought to feel the pangs of the new birth here, or made to repent of it forever. How dreadful it seems to me to hear him, I that am so afraid of death and so concerned lest I a'nt fit and prepared for it. What a dreadful thing it was that Mr Gridley died so! — too great, too big, too proud to learn any thing; would not let any minister pray with him; said he knew more than they could tell him, asked the news, and said he was going where he should hear no news'"

"Thus far landlady. As to landlord, he is happy and as big, as proud, as conceited as any nobleman in England; always calm and good natured and lazy, but the contemplation of his farm and his sons and his house and pasture and cows, his sound judgment as he thinks, and his great holiness, as well as that of his wife, keep him as erect in his thoughts as a noble or a prince."

During the years of the Revolutionary war there was located in the town of Barrington (R. I.) a tavern conducted by Henry Bowen. Connected with his popular hostelry was a country store, where all manner of articles for domestic u.se, from knitting needles to coffins, could be purchased. Both the tavern and the store were well patronized, and the old account books which

Bowen kept tell many an interesting story of life in the town during these eventful days.

It is not this, however, that is to be here noted, but it is the tavern keeper himself, for he was another of those ideal tavern keepers, and he exercised the prerogative of his position to its fullest extent and held public offices galore: he was collector of taxes, assessor of taxes, tithing man, Sunday constable, and sometimes he was called upon to act as moderator of the town meeting.

In addition to these he was a recruiting officer for the army, and was on various committees for furnishing clothing, arms and other supplies to the soldiers in the town. The thirst for public office grew in the tavern just as the thirst was allayed with that which was found at the tavern bar. John Adams noted it in his reminiscences, and said "if you sit the evening you will find the house full of people drinking drams, flip, toddy, carousing, swearing, but especially plotting with the landlord to get him at the next town meeting an election either for selectman or representative," while another contemporary writer has said, "the New Englanders all want to be Politicians, and therefore love the taverns and grog-bowl over which they do their business and drink from morning till night."

Lieutenant Joshua Fisher, who kept a Dedham tavern, was licensed in 1658 "to sell strong waters to relieve the inhabitants, being remote from Boston, for one year." In addition to his services to the town as purveyor of "strong waters," he was a surveyor, apothecary, and lieutenant in the militia.

Nat Bradley of Haverhill, who is described as one of the "handsomest and most popular hosts in all the region round and who tipped the scales at two hundred and fifty pounds," was a lieutenant in the militia. Thomas Fenner, who carried on a tavern "at his house in the woods" near Neutaconconit in Providence, was "Major for the main," which gave to him the command of all the militia on the mainland in Rhode Island. Besides this he was a justice of the peace, store keeper, and a surveyor of no mean ability.

Captain Ezra Lunt of Newburyport, who served through the whole Revolutionary war from Bunker Hill to Yorktown, and lived many years to recount his experiences, carried on a tavern, and was a man of the highest respectability. His service to the town was of a different character from those following a similar calling; it was unique. He was possessed of a fine voice, and regularly on Sundays attended service at the meeting house, and led the singing for many years, a leader in all that was spiritual.

Nathaniel Sparhawk of Cambridge, who in 1639 was licensed to keep a public house and "draw wine and strong water for Cambridge," was a deacon in the church, and doubtless contributed largely to the support of the minister, which some tavern keepers failed to do.

The colonial minister was settled over his parish at a stated annual salary. It was a simple arrangement to make, but far more difficult to keep, and rarely was he paid the amount agreed upon. A small part of this compensation was paid in money, but the greater part was in fish, butter, wood and other like commodities. All manner of excuses were made to the "tithing man" by the poor townsmen for neglecting' the minister's rate.

If there was any man in the town who would seem to be of sufficient ability to pay his part of the minister's rate without complaining, it was the tavern keeper, for he was the only business man in the community. Nevertheless he, too, evaded its payment. In 1674 John Ayers kept the historic tavern at Brookfield. Like most of his neighbors, he was in arrears for his tax for the parson's support, and was pressed to make payment. This he refused to do, giving as his reason "that he keeps the ordinary and has for time past and should be free from it."

It is not difficult to imagine why he took this position. Goodman Ayers' tavern was a near neighbor of the meeting house, for in 1714 when the new meeting house was built it was voted that it be set up in the "place where formerly the meeting house was built near old John Ayers home Lott lying near about the center of the town."

Now the tavern keeper usually furnished the sacrament wine and was often called upon to "accommodate the church occasions."

Goodman Ayer had in mind the many quarts and pints charged up against the meeting house on sacrament days and other occasions, and he failed to remember of any settlement. He also remembered the free use made of his place and stock on Sundays and other days, and the failure on the part of many of his guests to reimburse him for their entertainment, and he felt that he had contributed enough from his purse to the support of the meeting house and all therein contained.

In the town of Saugus there was a tavern kept by Mary Burke, which was a particularly popular place for sleighing parties in winter and picnic parties in summer. As was the custom in the latter days of the tavern the proprietors published, in the newspapers of the town, advertisements more or less enticing, calling attention to the attractions of their houses. Most of them are of the same general character, but that put out by Mistress Burke, and printed in the *Columbian Centinel*, is certainly interesting in one respect, her allusion to the interference of the Sabbath in the conduct of her place.

This notice was in the following words:

"Mary Burke,

Begs leave to inform her Friends and the Public in general that she shall continue to improve that commodious and agreeable situated house on said farm the present season where She proposes as far as in her power to accommodate those who please to favor her with their company.

Her house will be open every day in the week except the Sabbath — She is under the necessity of saying that on that day it will be shut up and no company entertained which she hopes her friends will excuse.

Her Larder will be constantly furnished with the choicest and most suitable provisions — her cellar with Liquors of the best quality — Her House with the best attendants she can procure — her stable with the best hay and

Provinder — And the favour of her guests studied to be gained and always gratefully acknowledged.

Fresh Pond is six miles from Boston; the roads good and improving; the Pond well stored with Fish, Boats and all necessary fishing apparatus for Ladies and gentlemen provided. The adjacent country furnishes Game — and the walks in its vicinity are rurally agreeable. April 11, 1792."

In fact it was all that human ingenuity could make it; an earthly paradise, as she reasoned it, except on the Sabbath. This was a source of regret to her and she took the only way left open and gave public notice that she must not be blamed that such a day occurred in the calendar. Licenses were frequently granted to women to conduct public houses, but there were usually some restrictions in such cases. The General Court of Massachusetts, on September 10, 1684, licensed several public houses in Boston; among these was a license to the wife of Nicholas Howard, who was "allowed to entertain Lodgers in the absence of her husband," but whether his return vitiated this license is not known.

Catherine Clark of Salem, a widow, was authorized in 1645 to keep a tavern if "She provides a fitt man that is godly to manage the business."

Salem people had a curious system surrounding the management of the tavern. The town deliberately licensed its tavern keepers to sell "bear & syder" on the Lord's day, but insisted that none but a man "that is godly" should manage such institutions. Perhaps, after all, there is more in this system than would at first appear, and that a solution of the liquor question can be had by a little experiment on the Salem plan.

From 1674 to 1686 Edward Anglers was regularly licensed to keep a public house of entertainment at Cambridge. Unlike most of those who occupied similar positions, he was a professional tavernkeeper and tapster. He had served an apprenticeship at the business in old England, where taverns flourished on every hand, and where the occupation was recognized as an "honest collinge." He had, too, grown old in this service, and his patronage and popularity were on the wane when he presented to the County Court at Cambridge in 1686 the following sorrowful appeal for a continuance of privileges.

"To the Honored Court assembled at Cambridge all prosperity wished:

These are to inform you that I was brought up in an honest collinge in ould England, where we sould all sorts of goods and strong waters without offence. I have bine now in this land forty nine yeres and upwards in this towne and have payd to the magistre and ministre and to towne charges, and all willingly; that I have helped to beare the burthen and heate of the daye and now I am 74 yeares and upwards yet I can abide in my shope and attend my collinge though little is to be gotten by any thinge I can by: that my trade will not maintayne my family and other charges of towne and countery and ministrye.

29

There being so many sellers that never served for a trade I desire that it might be no offence to any that I continue in that collinge I was brought up to, and may have yor leave to sell rome, it being a commodity sallabell and allowed to be brought into the country; and many that was formerly a commodity is not now. Hopeing you will grant me my request I rest yor servant

April 7 1686   **Edward Angiers**"

It was his last year at his trade, and his name disappears from the list of tavern keepers in Cambridge.

Another aged tapster of this town was John Stedman. For thirty-three years he had regularly been granted the privilege of "drawing wine" for the good people of Cambridge and others who entered his doors. Age seems to have dimmed his memory and blotted from it all recollection of that important preliminary which it was necessary to arrange before he could entertain visitors at the inn and not make himself liable. Age had also interfered with his personally conducting the business, and his place had been taken by his daughter and her husband, who unconsciously, perhaps, had gone about it without making any arrangements with the County Court for the privilege. It so happened that in the fall of 1690 "his daughter Sharp" was detected by one of the constables in the act of selling rum without a license, and she was summoned to Court to answer for this illegal proceeding. Then John Stedman came to the rescue and presented this ingenious petition to the Court to excuse his daughter's indiscretion. If it were not for his years, the excuse that he did not know "when and where he ought to apply himself" for a license would excite some suspicion, especially after the habit of thirtythree years. This was his plea:

"To the honored County Court sitting by adjournment at Charlestown 24 8m 1690:

The petition of John Stedman of Cambridge aged 88 sheweth That your petitioner, as is well known hath had a license to sell Rum for many years past, which never was discontinued till the Revolution since which he would have sought for the renewal of it had he had the least notice when or where he ought to apply himself for it or that any others renewed there's That your petitioner wonders that his daughter Sharp should be summoned to this Court for selling Rum without license, she never having sold any at Cambridge on her own or her husbands account but upon the sole and proper account and by the order of your petitioner, who is well assured that he hath never given cause to be dealt with in extremity he having never bin behindhand in paying for his draft or in serving his country to his power.

Your petitioner therefore praies that his daughter Sharp may no further be molested or discouraged from the dutiful and charitable assistance of your petitioner for his support and comfort in his extream old age and that a license may be granted him as formerly. So praies your humble servant

John Stedman."

The tavern keeper who run the ferry or whose house was located beside it was often accused of sacrificing the traveller's comfort and happiness for his own private gain. Colonel Israel Angell, a veteran of the Revolution, and one of the bravest and most fearless commanders in the war, made a trip to the Ohio Valley in the year 1788. He kept a diary of his travels through the wilderness, and, in his journey homeward came to the ferry at Paulus Hook in New Jersey, and under the date of October 2d he gives his experience with the ferryman who it seems also kept a house for the entertainment of travellers: "here we found no boat, they all being over at York," he says, "but the ferryman told us there would be a boat over immediately here we waited until 9 o'clock then he was kind enough to tell us we might put up our horses as there would be no boat that night, and having a hint by a gentleman that came to the ferry with me that he was a man frequently guilty of serving travelers such tricks to oblige them to spend their money with him. However I had seen too much of mankind to be catched by him I asked him what he would ask me to keep my hors the night he said 2 shillings. So I bid him good night and tho' a stranger thought I would take my chance rode about ½ a mile back where I got good entertainment for ¼ part of what that rascal would demand of me."

William Turpin of Providence, besides being the innkeeper and caterer to the town council, which regularly assembled at his house, was the schoolmaster, the first in the town of which there is any record. There is nothing remaining to show what his charges were to patrons of his tavern, but if they were no more exorbitant than his charges for schooling there was little opportunity for "higgling" over the bills which were presented to his guests. On the 11th day of June, 1684, Turpin executed an indenture with William Hawkins and his wife Lydia, "in which he covenanted to furnish Peregrine Gardiner with board and school for one year for six pounds; forty shillings of which in beef and pork, pork at two pence, and beef at three pence half penny, per lb; twenty shillings in corn, at two shillings per bushel, and the balance in silver money." For this consideration the lad was to be instructed in reading and writing.

Turpin was an excellent penman and his services were constantly in demand by his neighbors. When Sir Edmund Andros came into power in New England and proceeded to assess a tax on everything above ground and some things below, he levied a rate on every male person in his jurisdiction of the age of sixteen years and upwards of "one shilling and eight pence by the Head," and the assessors were directed to bring in "fairly written the just Number of the Male Persons listed." For this purpose the services of Turpin were employed. This old list is yet preserved, written in the bold, clear and elegant hand of this old tavern keeper.

It would be difficult to name a scene in early colonial life in which the tavern keeper did not act a part, but the curtain has been rung down and the Colonial Boniface is but a memory.

Chapter Three - The Tavern Sign and Name

A conspicuous feature of the tavern was its sign, which hung either on or in front of the house. On this was depicted some emblem or device suggestive of the name which the tavern bore. In some cases there was only a name painted upon a rudely constructed sign board attached to a wooden arm projecting from the tavern itself or from a post; sometimes a convenient tree which shaded the hostelry was utilized for this purpose. In the larger settlements these signs were often more elaborately constructed and were made with an iron arm, with some attempt at ornamentation.

One old tavern keeper has preserved the cost of his sign, and from his old account book it appears that the "Sign with the arm to hang it on" cost fifteen shillings. This was the sign at Henry Bowen's tavern at Barrington, and the old post from which it swung, is standing now. From another account book there is the entry "for making a sign five shillings," while for "Iron work for sign as we agreed" three shillings is charged. These were probably not very elaborate sign boards.

The history of sign boards dates back to the time of the Greeks and Romans, and even the ancient Egyptians used signs of like character to attract attention to the wares which they exposed for sale.

It is from the Roman tavern signs that the English derived the earliest symbol used for this purpose, the bush, and from the use of which the proverb "Good wine needs no Bush" had its origin. Shirley, in his *Masque of the Triumph of Peace*, says: "Taverns are quickly set up, it is but hanging out a bush at a nobleman's or an alderman's gate and 'tis made instantly." Sometimes a sign board was displayed in addition to the bush. An old French ballad contains these words:

"The tavern opened
with signboard and bush
The landlady's hair neatly dressed
Tied up in a knot."

In modern times this emblem has been used in the western mining camps and settlements to indicate the location of the grocery or bar-room. The bush itself was discarded as more prosperous times came to the inn, and if there was enough in the name to preserve it, the sign was lettered "Ivy Bush" or "Green Bush," and this name given to the house. The ale stake or ale pole finds its origin in the sign of the bush.

There was, until within a few years, an old tavern in the town of Barrington, a few miles beyond Bowen's tavern, bearing the name "Green Bush tavern," a ponderous wooden sign hung from a post before the house, on which was painted a tree or bush.

The custom of naming the tavern and attaching thereto the sign was brought to New England from Holland and the mother country, where taverns flourished everywhere, and where sign boards had reached a high grade of artistic merit, and had also become a great nuisance on account of their number and enormous proportions. They never reached the extent in New England that they did in Old England.

In France, too, a sign for the tavern was prescribed by an ordinance of Louis XIV, which said "Tavernkeepers must put up synboards and a bush = Nobody shall be allowed to open a tavern in the said city and its suburbs without having a sign and a bush."

A curious rhyme printed in the *British Apollo,* in 1710, throws some light on the number and kinds of such sign boards in London at that period, as well as the curious combinations of names which had been bestowed upon the public house, for the writer says:

"I'm amazed at the signs,
As I pass through the town,
To see the odd mixture,
A Magpie and Crown,
The Whale and the Crow,
The Razor and Hen,
The Leg and Seven Stars,
The Axe and the Bottle,
The Tun and the Lute,
The Eagle and Child,
The Shovel and Boot."

These signs had been displayed by virtue of royal authority for, in the time of Charles I., the charter of London contained this clause relative to sign boards:

"And further, we do give and grant to the said Mayor, and Commonalty, and Citizens of the said city, and their successors, that it may and shall be lawful to the Citizens of the same city and any of them, for the time being, to expose and hang in and over the streets, and ways, and alleys of the said city and suburbs of the same, signs, and posts of signs, affixed to their houses and shops for the better finding out such citizen's dwellings, shops, arts or occupations, without impediment, molestation, or interruption of his heirs or successors."

The derivation of most of these curious combinations, so common in England, are unknown, and it is impossible to even conjecture. Some of them, however, are known, and of a few the origin has been assumed with great probability that the assumption is correct. "The Leg and Seven Stars" was merely a deviation from the League and Seven Stars or Seven United Provinces. "The Axe and the Bottle" was a transposition of Battle Axe, and the reason for these departures from the original is explained thus: When these sign boards from long exposure to storms, sunshine, and varying climatic influences, became indistinct and worn, the sign painter, to whom they were turned over for repairs, was not always careful to replace the words as he had found them. There was no prescribed rule of orthography, and if the sign painter had covered the whole surface with paint, blotting out the original name or device, he would depend on his memory, often treacherous, to replace it. The sign "Goat and Compasses," is said to have originally read, "God encompasseth us." "The Bag of Nails," a tavern at Chelsea, England, was but a corruption of the word "Bacchanals." The "Bull and Mouth" was also a corruption of the name "Boulogne Mouth" which tavern was located at the harbor of Boulogne. These curious names and combinations of words which had been inscribed upon the tavern signs, formed the groundwork for many sprightly ditties, and the seventeenth century songs and ballads were full of allusions to them, woven into rollicking rhyme. There is one called "The Mail Coach Guard," where the names of the taverns are ingeniously introduced into the verse:

> At each inn on the road I a welcome could find: —
>   At the *Fleece* I'd my skin full of ale;
> The *Two Jolly Brewers* were just to my mind;
>   At the *Dolphin* I drank like a whale.
> Tom Tun at the *Hogshead* sold pretty good stuff;
>   They'd capital flip at the *Boar;*
> And when at the *Angel* I'd tippled enough,
>   I went to the *Devil* for more.
> Then I'd always a sweetheart so snug at the *Car;*
>   At the *Rose* I'd a lily so white;
> Few planets could equal sweet Nan at the *Star*,
>   No eyes ever twinkled so bright.
> I've had many a hug at the sign of the *Bear;*
>   In the *Sun* courted morning and noon;
> And when night put an end to my happiness there,
>   I'd a sweet little girl in the *Moon.*
> To sweethearts and ale I at length bid adieu,
>   Of wedlock to set up the sign;
> *Hand-in-hand* the *Good Woman* I look for in you,
>   And the *Horns* I hope ne'er be mine.
> Once guard to the mail, I'm now guard to the fair;
>   But though my commission's laid down;
> Yet while the *King's Arms* I'm permitted to bear;
>   Like a *Lion* I'll fight for the *Crown.*

Following the custom of the mother country, the legislative authority of the colonies made similar orders to those in vogue at home, relative to the placing of a sign when the tavern was licensed. The sign thus became evidence of a regularly authorized house of entertainment, and when, for any reason, the license of a tavern keeper or disposer of liquors was revoked, it was followed by taking down the sign, which finds reference in Massinger's *A New Way to Pay Old Debts.*

"For this gross fault I here do damn thy licence,
  Forbidding thee even to tap or draw;
  For instantly I will in mine own person,
  Command the constables to pull down thy sign."

Massachusetts, by an act of the General Court in 1710, made provision for just this course of procedure, and gave to the sheriff or deputy the power and authority, when a taverner had his license revoked for any irregularity, "to cause his sign to be taken down."

It cannot be said that there was a great variety of curious combinations of names in early New England tavern signs; they were mostly commonplace and lacked originality. But what the taverns lacked in this respect was made up in the good cheer which they afforded.

After the Revolutionary war this condition was changed, and these signs had a certain originality that was unique, for the American eagle was everywhere displayed, holding the British lion in chains, or with wings extended, and alleged portraits of General Washington, Lafayette and other prominent personages connected with the war, according to the locality, were seen on every hand.

On the third of November, 1766, John Adams wrote in his diary, "Set off with my wife for Salem, stopped half an hour at Boston, crossed the ferry, and at three o'clock arrived at Hills', the tavern at Maiden, the sign of the Rising Eagle."

Ten years later the eagle had arisen, and on

"lofty pinions plumed its flight to hights sublime."

The annals of early New England contain few references to the sign itself, although the fact that they were in common use is abundantly proven. A tavern might have a name, but it did not necessarily follow that it had a sign. The earliest reference to the sign that has been found is in Salem, where, in 1645, a license was granted with the proviso that there "be set up some inoffensive sign obvious for direction to strangers." Ten years later the Colonial legislature of Rhode Island licensed eight persons in different parts of the colony to keep houses of entertainment, and provided that each person so appointed "for ye said imployment shall cause to be sett out a convenient signe at ye most perspicuous place of ye saide house, thereby to give notice to strangers that it is a house of public entertainment, and this is to be done with all convenient speed."

When Abraham Stafford opened his tavern at Salem some years before the Revolutionary war, he advertised the attractions of his place, prominent among which he mentions "an elegant sign of King George the third." After the war all signs of royalty were removed from both public and private buildings. In the town of Newburyport, the Wolfe Tavern, whereon hung a sign bearing an alleged likeness of General Wolfe, continued to display this sign. Whether this was an inadvertence or whether the landlord disliked to discard a totem that had so long been connected with his establishment is not positively known; it is said, however, that it was through accident that it was allowed to remain; nevertheless it produced a bitter tirade of criticism, and the newspapers openly denounced the landlord for permitting it to swing and declared its existence "in the very centre of the place to be an insult to the inhabitants of this truly republican town."

The Ames Tavern at Dedham was conducted by Nathaniel Ames, the celebrated Almanack maker, who began catering to the weary traveller about the year 1735. The tavern, however, had been in operation for many years, the first license for it being dated 1658. The sign which landlord Ames put out before his establishment was unique; besides, it had a history, or rather it illustrated an episode in his family history, and was the source of some trouble to him.

In the settlement of the estate of his son, Fisher Ames, there was brought about a suit at law, which was before the courts for many years, much to the disgust and annoyance of the tavern keeper. At last the court decided in favor of Landlord Ames, but so disgusted had he become at the annoying delay that he thought he would indulge in a little fun at the expense of the court. Worthington, in his History of Dedham, tells the story in these words: "Dr. Ames, although the successful party, expressed his dislike at the conduct of the dissenting judges (one of whom was Paul Dudley, the chief justice), by causing the whole court to be painted on the large sign board of his tavern, sitting in great state in their large wigs, each judge being clearly recognized. An open book was before them, underneath which was written, *Province Laws.*" The dissenting judges were represented with their backs turned towards the book. The court hearing of the sign sent the sheriff to bring it before them. Dr. Ames heard the order given, being then in Boston, and by good luck and hard riding, had just time enough to pull down his sign before the sheriff arrived at Dedham."

Sam Briggs, in his volume *The Almanack of Nathaniel Ames, 1726-1775*, presents a full-page illustration of this sign, which he says "is a copy of the original sketch made by Dr. Ames for the sign, the sketch having been found recently among his papers."

On the elevated bench are the five Judges, Benjamin Lynde, Richard Saltonstall, Paul Dudley, Stephen Sewall and John Gushing. Lynde and Dudley are represented with their backs turned.

Around a table in front of the bench are six figures, one of whom is standing. Over the head of the Chief Justice, the central figure, is the arms of Great Britain, while above this is the inscription, "Nearest Akin to Fisher." Underneath the whole is "August 18, 1749."

Upon this original sketch of the sign the following words are written:

"Sir: — I wish I could have some talk on Y above subject, being the bearer waits for an answer shall only observe Mr. Greenwoods thinks yt can not be done under £40, old tenor."

This was quite a price for a sign, but he doubtless paid it willingly for the sake of gratifying this desire to lampoon the Court.

A most imposing sign was that erected to attract travelers to the tavern at Barre, Mass. It consisted of two upright poles or masts about five feet apart and about twenty feet in height. A weather vane was at the top of each pole. From a bar near the top, reaching from pole to pole, hung the ponderous wooden sign of the Barre Hotel. This structure was built upon an open green space directly in front of the tavern.

It was not unusual for a taverner to add underneath the symbol on his sign, or upon the opposite side, some enticing words, calling attention to the excellence of his wares or the homelike comforts of his place.

A taverner whose patronage was largely among seafaring men would display this couplet:

"Coil up your ropes and anchor here
 Till better weather doth appear."

Another sign, put out by Landlord Collins, at his place in Knockholt, in Kent (England), had this poetical effusion:

"Charles Collins liveth here
Sells rum, brandy, gin and beer;
I make this board a little wider,
To let you know I sell good cyder."

Landlord Dale of the "King's Head," at Strutton, near Ipswich (England), had the following rhyme upon his sign board:

"Good people, stop, and pray walk in,
 Here's foreign brandy, rum and gin,
 And what is more, good purl and ale,
 Are both sold here by old Nat Dale."

Another tavern, at the sign of the "Oak," had this:

"I am an oak and not a yew.
So drink a cup with good John Pugh."

(The most curious of these rhyming sign boards had two rhymes, one on either side of the board. The tavern, where it was set up, was at the foot of a steep hill. The traveller, therefore, upon approaching it from the level roadway, was first greeted with these words staring at him from the swinging sign:

"Before you do this hill go up,
 Stop and drink a cheering cup."

While the traveller, upon descending the hill, read:

"You're down the hill all danger's past.
 Stop and drink a cheerful glass."

And thus mine host caught the wayfarer both ways.

On one of the window panes which formerly did service in the Red Horse Tavern, at Sudbury, Mass., the "Wayside Inn" of Longfellow, there is written these words:

"What do you think,
 Here is good drink,
 Perhaps you may not know it;
 If not in haste, do stop and taste
 You merry folks will shew it."

Underneath this is written the name 'of the author and the date.
"Wm. Mollineux, Jr., Esq.,
24th June, 1774, Boston."

Some years ago this window glass was removed from its setting and placed in a frame for safer keeping.

The sign on an old tavern at Medford represented two men bowing and shaking hands, and the house, therefore, acquired the names of the Palavers Tavern and the Salutation Tavern.

These do not seem to have been pleasing names to the landlord, and as it was a most popular place, being on the main road between Boston and Salem, the landlord discarded this sign and designed another, representing a fountain pouring punch into a large bowl, and gave to the house the name. Fountain Tavern. It is said that the landlord aimed to make this house a little superior to the other houses of its character and provided some extra attractions to the place.

Two large elm trees shaded the house and the grounds around it, and there were built in the branches of each of these great trees substantial platforms which were connected with each other and with the house by wooden stairs and bridges. In these leafy retreats the patrons of the house would repair during the hot summer days, and sip their punch and other liquors and discuss current questions. It was also a favorite resort for tea parties and social gatherings, when such uncommon beverages, to the tavern, as tea and "choca" would be supplied. A tavern bearing a similar name, the "Salutation," was in Boston at the junction of North street and Salutation Alley. It was a favorite haunt for seafaring men and ship builders, and Drake in his "Old Boston Taverns," says. "it became the fusion between the leading Whig politicians and the shipwrights. More than sixty influential mechanics attended the first meeting in 1772, at which Dr. Warren drew up a code of bylaws. Some leading mechanic, however, was always chosen to be the moderator.

The 'caucus' as it began to be called, continued to meet in this place until after the destruction of the tea, when for greater secrecy, it became advisable to transfer the sittings to another place, and then the "Green Dragon," on Union street, was selected." The sign at the "Salutation" was similar to that at the Medford hostelry, and it was more generally known as the "Palavers." The "Green Dragon" was located not far from where the tablet, with the carved representation of a dragon, is placed on Union street.

There was yet another sign which the tavern keeper displayed, but not as an attraction to his house, for it was not upon the outside but within doors, and in the most conspicuous place in the tap-room. "Mind your P's and Q's," was the motto for the tavern keeper. The habit of marking down upon the tavern book the charges for the liquors furnished, often resulted in a material loss to the tapster. He therefore took such precautions as were consistent with his policy of management, and adopted such rules as experience had found necessary, to compel payment for the liquors which he furnished at his bar. Rarely was he arbitrary in enforcing his rules, but on the other hand, diplomatic and gentlemanly in bringing to the attention of patrons, by his tap-room sign, the important rule, of paying as you go.

These signs were worded in such a sly way that they were more apt to produce a laugh than a frown. No one could keep a long face as he watched this sign and drank of Greadly's beer.

"Greadly Bob, he does live here,
   And sells a pot of good strong beer;
 His liquors 's good, his measure 's just.
   But Bob 's so poor he cannot trust."

A smile was bound to broaden the face of him who read:

"Within this hive we're all alive,
   With whisky sweet as honey;
 If you are dry, step in and try.
   But don't forget the money."

Or this:

"My liquor's good,
   My measure's just;
 Excuse me, sirs!
   I cannot trust."

A picture of a dead dog was sometimes used, under which was written:

"Died last night: Poor Trust.
 Who killed him? Bad Pay."

Another form used was a board fashioned into the shape of a tombstone, set in one corner of the room, whereon was inscribed:

"This monument is erected to the memory of Mr. Trust, who was some time since most shamefully and cruelly murdered by a villain called Credit, who is prowling about, both in town and country, seeking whom he may devour."

Another will suffice to illustrate this form of the tavern sign:

"The rule of this house, and it can't be unjust,
  Is to pay on delivery, and not to give trust;
  I've trusted many to my sorrow.
  Pay to-day, I'll trust to-morrow."

A word well understood by all travellers had its origin in the tavern, and it is more closely identified with similar institutions today than in any other place. In early clays one of the accessories of the great room of the tavern was a small box nailed to the wall. It had at the top a small opening wherein pieces of money might be dropped; on the face of this box there was printed in letters easily read, "To Insure Promptness," and it was expected that guests would drop in this receptacle such amounts as their inclinations prompted.

The money thus collected was taken out from time to time and divided among the servants in the house. It was not infrequent that some *attache* of the tavern would remind a careless guest of this box, and in so doing would point with his finger in its direction and speak the first letter of the words, T. I. P. It gradually became known as the Tip box, and later as a tip. The box finally disappeared, and its place is now taken by the outstretched palm, and though the word is seldom spoken, the eye of the palmist speaks a language plainer than any tongue.

To give all the names which were bestowed upon the taverns and which were painted upon their swinging signs would be an endless task. The earlier houses bore names which were mostly copied from old English inns. The "King's Arms" and the "King's Head" were common names in New England previous to the Revolution. Boston had taverns with these names and so had London. In connection with these the following story is told: "A certain amorous king, while attending a public court ball, was noticed to be particularly attentive to a fair young damsel; one of the courtiers, wishing to retire to some tavern for refreshment, inquired of another what house he would recommend, who wittily replied that he had better not go to the 'King's Arms,' as they were full, but that the 'King's Head' was empty."

The "St. George," at Roxbury, had its representative in the "George," "St. George," and "St. George and the Dragon" all over England. Tilton's tavern, at Portsmouth, had a likeness of the Marquis of Rockingham upon its sign. Near Faneuil Hall, Boston, in 1773, was the "General Wolfe," and at the same time there was swinging before the tavern in Brooklyn, Conn., where General Israel Putnam had formerly catered to travelers, a sign bearing the same name. This old sign is now preserved in the collection of the Connecticut Historical Society. It is made of yellow pine, painted alike on both sides, with a full length portrait of General Wolfe in scarlet uniform.

The "Admiral Vernon" was a popular name, and since this distinguished individual was generally known as "Old Grog," there appears to be more reason in using this name upon a tavern sign than any other personage that has yet been mentioned.

A bunch of grapes was a common sign; tradesmen and taverners used it, and it was as often in front of a dry goods store as a house of entertainment.

At the Essex Institute, in Salem, is a portion of the sign which formerly hung at the "Bunch of Grapes," on State street, Boston, a famous coaching station in the days of the Boston and Providence stages. It is made of clay, moulded and baked, and is said to have been brought from England.

There is an old tavern in the pleasant town of Paxton, Mass., that has long been a most popular resort for travellers, and today its popularity is as universal as it was in the days before the Revolution, when its doors were first opened. Unlike most of the old taverns throughout New England, this establishment never sheltered the illustrious Washington, and this is a distinction which, with the traditional stories clustering around most of these ancient hostelries, makes it unique.

Swinging to and fro in front of the house, just as it has swung for more than a century, is the old sign of the Paxton Inn. It is about three feet wide and four feet long, and has painted upon one side "a picture representing Lord Cornwallis and Charles Paxton shaking hands across a well loaded table, at which they appear to be dining." On the reverse is another picture, a group of vegetables, such as are commonly used in a good dinner. This sign, when it was first put out to attract the attention of the wayfarer, is said to have cost one hundred dollars.

The town takes its name from this same Charles Paxton, whose portrait adorns the sign, and who, in ante-revolutionary days, was the marshal of the Admiralty Court at Boston. He is described as "an intriguing politician and a despicable sycophant," and his official acts made him so obnoxious to the people of Boston that he was hung in effigy upon the Liberty Tree which formerly stood at the corner of Essex and Washington streets.

When the town was named, as an inducement to bestow upon it his own name, Paxton promised to give the town a bell for the meeting house, but he failed to make good his promise. The name thus given was greatly disliked by the townspeople, and a petition was finally presented to the General Court of Massachusetts, praying that it be changed to a "name more agreeable;" the change, however, was never made. Through all this season of bitter denunciation which followed, the portrait of the town's namesake swung idly in the wind, and there are few, probably, to-day, who realize how utterly despised and detested was the person whose image now looks down upon the good people of Paxton.

The sign which formerly hung before John Duggan's hostelry, in Boston, on what is now Corn Court, had on it a portrait of John Hancock. It is said to resemble one of Copley's portraits of the governor. Landlord Duggan was a friend and admirer of Hancock, and when he was elected governor of the Commonwealth, had this sign painted. Upon the death of this prominent personage Duggan caused the sign to be appropriately draped in mourning emblems. It swung for many years over the narrow alley until one day, in a high wind, it was blown from its fastenings and killed a passer by. When it was replaced it was securely nailed to the side of the building, where it remained for some time, and was then taken down and deposited in Memorial Hall, at Lexington, where it now remains.

In seaport towns the "Ship" was a name much used, and in England there was scarcely a seaport but what had a Ship inn or tavern, and the name is joined in more combinations than any given to such places. These produced signs which were particularly attractive to seafaring men, and it was on this account that the name was used, for there was the "Ship," "Ship and Anchor," "Ship and Bell," "Ship and Blue Coat Boy," "Ship and Castle," "Ship and Fox," "Ship and Notchblock," "Ship and Pilot Boat," "Ship and Plough," "Ship and Punch-bowl," "Ship and Rainbow," "Ship and Shovel," "Ship and Star," "Ship and Whale," "Ship at Anchor," "Ship Friends," Ship in Full Sail," "Ship in Distress," "Ship in Dock," and "Ship on Launch." Every condition of the ship seems to have been represented in the name of the tavern where Jack could find his comfort and cheer. Add to either one of these names such an alluring couplet as

"Coil up your ropes and anchor here
 Till better weather doth appear,"

and there was enough to attract Jack until the ship sailed.

Such taverns often served as a shipping office for privateers, and the ship's articles were here left for the signatures of those who "have a mind" to ship. Notice of such is found in the *Boston Post Boy*, in June, 1762, in the following words:

"Now Bound on a **CRUIZE** of Six Months

Against his Majesty's Enemies, The Brigantine *Tartar*, A Prime Sailer mounting Fourteen Six Pounders, Twenty culverins, and will carry One Hundred and Twenty Men, Commanded by William Augustus Peck.

"**All Gentlemen Seamen** and able bodied Landmen, who have a mind to make their Fortunes, and are inclined to take a cruize in said Vessel, by applying to the King's Head Tavern at the North End may view the Articles which are more advantageous to the Ship's Company than ever were before offered in this Place."

There is a certain grim humor in this advertisement for "gentlemen sailors." It was all pleasant enough to address them as such on shore, in the taproom of the tavern, especially when there was a desire for their services. But by what title did bluff Captain Peck address these "gentlemen sailors" when the good ship *Tartar* was in mid-ocean and the nearest land four miles from the vessel's keel?

With the advent of the newspaper a wide awake landlord would give, notice of the attractions of his establishment by inserting in the columns of the paper a suitable advertisement. Nathaniel Ames, the doctor-astronomer tavernkeeper at Dedham, used his Almanack at times for his advertising medium, and since his almanack had almost as much circulation as any newspaper of the period, the good qualities of his hostelry were widely made known. His notice was in the following words in the Almanack for 1751:

"**Advertisement.**

These are to signify to all persons that travel the great Post-Road, South-West from Boston, That I keep a House of Publick Entertainment Eleven Miles from Boston, at the Sign of the Sun. If they want Refreshment, and see cause to be my Guests, they shall be well entertained at a reasonable Rate,

N. AMES."

The next year this notice appeared:

"The Affairs of my House are of a Publick Nature, and therefore I hope may be mentioned here without offence to my *Readers:*

The Sign I advertised last year by Reasons of some little Disappointments, is not put up, but the thing intended to be signified by it is to be had according to said Advertisement.

And I beg Leave further to add, that if any with a view of Gain to themselves, or Advantage to their Friends, have reported Things of my House in contradiction to the aforesaid Advertisement, I would only have those whom they would influence consider that when the Narrator is not honest, is not an Eye or Ear Witness, can't trace his Story to the original, has it only by Hear-Say, a thousand such Witnesses are not sufficient to hang a Dog & I hope no Gentleman that travels the Road will have his Mind biased against my House by such idle Reports."

There was a rival institution in the town conducted by one Gay, and he had doubtless circulated derogatory statements relative to the Ames establishment. Perhaps on account of a dinner party which landlord Ames seems to have attracted to his own table after arrangements had already been made with landlord Gay.

Henry Rice of the "Golden Ball," at Providence, gave notice of his place by the following, published in the *Providence Gazette,* December 13, 1783. The "Golden Ball" later became known as the Mansion House, and has been open to the public from that day to this.

"Henry Rice begs Leave most respectfully to inform the Public that he has removed from the House he lately occupied opposite Messrs. Joseph and William Russell to a New House which he has just finished in the Back street, at the **Golden Ball** opposite the State House. As his house was erected purposely for an Inn, and is well furnished, he flatters himself it will afford every Comfort and Accommodation to the weary Traveller. He has also erected very large and commodious Stabling Sheds for Carriages, and other Out-Buildings.

The greatest attention will be paid to those who may please to honor him with their Commands, and he will be particularly happy in waiting on his old Customers in his new Situation."

The early numbers of the New England newspapers contain many of these curious advertisements, and of the comfortable surroundings of these houses, and the "good things to eat and other things "many distinguished persons have left abundant testimony. The old tavern signs, however, have mostly disappeared, and are now seldom seen except among the carefully treasured relics of by-gone days in the collections of museums and historical societies.

Chapter Four - The Tavern and Training Day

OF all the busy and important days which the tavern saw, the busiest was on Training Days or Squadron Days, as they were called in the New Haven Colony. From early morning till nine o'clock in the evening the tavern was thronged with a jolly, good-natured crowd, brought thither by the festivities of the day. Training days were regulated by law, and usually occurred eight times a year, although special, extra and voluntary trainings sometimes took place, either of the whole military force in the town or of separate companies of the train bands. They were usually held on Saturdays, and all males between sixteen and sixty not physically incapacitated were required to perform military service. Saturday made a good day for the "training," as the week's work was practically at an end, and the rest and refreshment of the Sabbath was gladly welcomed after the rigors of the military evolutions and involutions and other exertions incident thereto.

The Great and General Court of Massachusetts, in 1631, "Ordered that every first Friday in every month there shall be a general training of those that inhabit Charlestown Mistick and the Newtown at a convenient place about the Indian wigwams the training to begin at one of the clock in the afternoon." This location was perhaps selected so that the importance of this military aggregation would be gravely impressed upon the minds of the red heathen. In 1637, however, this number was reduced to eight, for in the planting and harvesting season there was too much depending upon the labors in the field to devote even a day to the duty of training. Each member of the train band was required by law to equip himself with a "musket (firelock or matchlock or snaphaunce) a pair of bandoliers, a powder pouch with bullets, a sword, a belt, a worm, a scourer, a rest and a knapsack." Bandoliers were most essential to the soldier's comfort, for they supported the gun and other heavy equipments which he was obliged to carry, and relieved him of that weight, which always seemed to accumulate as the hours of the day wore on.

In the New Haven Colony it was ordered that each soldier should furnish "a good serviceable gun, a good sword, bandoliers, a rest, one pound of good gun powder, four pounds of bullets either fitted for his gun or pistol bullets four fathom of match fit for service with every matchlock and four or five good flints fitted for every fire lock piece all in good order and ready for any suddain occasion service or view."

In 1658 the town of Eastham (Mass.) appropriated a sufficient amount of money to pay a bill which had been presented, including these charges:

For a drum for the military company	3	0	0
For pikes	2	16	4

And in 1681 it was "voted that the military company should be filled by such of the inhabitants as were able to bear arms, and that every soldier be furnished with a sword or cutlass as well as a gun, and that a part of the company should carry their arms to meeting on the Lord's day."

Early in the morning of training day the townsmen equipped with the arms and accoutrements required by the law, set out for the rendezvous, often many miles from their homes.

The occasion was in the nature of a holiday; every one laid aside his work and repaired to the training field or to the place where the militia had its headquarters. No event in colonial life brought together so many people as the training. On this account it was considered a convenient time to hold a town meeting, and the records of most New England towns contain the proceedings of meetings held "att a training."

At a town meeting in Boston, March 14, 1698, it was "voted that Rumny Marsh and Muddi rever Each place haue Liberty to Chuse an Assessor to set with the Selectmen, for the making of their Own Rates. Each place is to make their chose of their sd Assessor. On their first Traning Day and when chosen to bring them on ye day of a publick Town meeting to be confirmed by the Town."

A fine was imposed on each member of the train band who failed to respond at roll call; there were, however, certain persons who were exempt from this duty. Ministers, colony and town officers and some others, besides "magistrates teaching elders and deacons of churches were allowed each of them a man free on Training days." Ship carpenters, fishermen and millers were also excused from attendance. Millers were excused "because in attending tide mills they were often obliged to be at work through the night."

In Providence it was "ordered that those farms which are one mile off the town alone shall have liberty to leave one man at home on the trayneing dayes." This was to protect the home and family from any excursion that the Indians might plan if there was no one about the place to defend the household.

The money received for fines was sometimes used to "be disposed of in powder and shot that they may set up marks to shoot at or may furnish themselves for their military exercises."

The fines thus imposed for delinquency in training were kept account of by the clerk of the company, and if the person owing it did not settle promptly, his neglect was the subject of judicial investigation and action.

Among the old papers formerly belonging to Major Thomas Fenner, so frequently referred to, are many which illustrate the custom and practice in the military companies in the early part of the eighteenth century, and he has preserved the record of the consideration of certain cases of this character in the following memorandum:

"At a Court of magistrates held in Providence at the house of Mr. William Turpin the fifth of January 1707

Captain Silvanus Scott Complainant against Thomas Cumstock for three days Neglect for not Cuming to training & Daniel Coumstock two days neglect for not cuming to training, there being no efects to be found this Cas is brought before us Acording as the Law directs."

He has also left plenary evidence of how he collected these fines, when he was both tavern keeper and captain of the train band, for he charged their indebtedness for absence on training days right in with such other charges as he had against his men on the book of accounts at the tavern, and among such entries is the following:

"Benj Wright debtor for 4 Barils of cyder and twelve shillings to excuse him from Training two years past."

The soldiers were not always required to march and countermarch and go through the simple manual of arms then in vogue on such occasions; their services were put to more useful purposes, and Captain Turner's company of Lynn, having come together at the regular training in 1634, marched in a body down to Nahant and spent the day hunting wolves, over the very territory now occupied by those magnificent summer villas that cluster upon the point.

The officers of the Train band were usually elected on Training days, and this fact was always born in mind by the townsmen as well as by those who composed the company, for it was the custom for the officers and particularly the captain to treat, not only his company but every one else. Whenever the captain happened to be a tavern keeper, and this was so often the case that it was bound to happen, he, particularly, was expected to be "generous in treating."

"We had our Training and Treeting &c the company was all here about loo we had 1 88 people here to dinner," wrote Samuel Pierce of Dorchester, an old tavern keeper, in his diary, and

"a traine band captain eke was he."

With so much "training and treeting," many of those who attended the day's festivities took far many more steps in their journey homeward than they had in coming.

We have the "score" charged against one Warwick (R. I.) man, which includes his town meeting day and Training day potations:

46

" Joyned with Moses Lippit	o	o	1
halfe a pint the same day	o	o	2
halfe a pint with Capt Jones	o	o	4
Town meeting day at night half a pint	o	o	4
that day wee shot at markes 2 half pints	o	o	8
2 half pints more	o	o	8
training day one quart	o	1	o
one quart home	o	1	o
you say I had one pint more	o	o	6
halfe a pint	o	o	3

The charges on training day show that he kept up the customs of the day, and it is not surprising that his recollection of just the amount taken was a little clouded; he had confidence, however, in the tavern keeper that the charges were correct, for in the old pig-skin covered account book from which these items are taken, the charges are all marked "paid."

On another old tavern account book are found these charges made on a "Training day."

"Johnathan Bosworth, Dr.

To 1 Dinner 1s 4d To 1 Cake ginger- bread 4d Training day	o	1	8 "

" Viall Allen, Dr.

To 1 Dinner Training day 1s 4d To 1 mug flip 9d	o	2	1 "

"Samuel Bosworth, Dr.

To ye Club Training day 3s 11d To Cash 12s	o	15	11 "

While others are made up of dinners, mugs of flip, gills of cherry rum, mugs of cider, and quarts of "good New England Rum."

These meetings of the train bands were as full of politics as an egg is of meat, and the man who could successfully pilot a candidate for office through the winding channels of such a meeting was a person of tact, genius and ability, a diplomat of such overpowering influence that his services were soon transferred to the more important and wider fields of usefulness in the town meetings.

The train bands were called together for elections by such an order as this:

"You James Thornton Corporail of the third Companie or Traine Band in providence these are in his maiesties name William the third over England Scotland France and Ireland to Require you to warne all the Trained soulders of said Compani to Apere with their Armes upon the 25th of this instant May 1702 at the now dwelling house of Thomas Fenner by 10 of the clock on the fore noon then and there to chose theire Military officers for the next insewing year fail not as you will Answer the contrari given by me

At another election of this company trouble was precipitated by one of the factions and the result shows that some of the methods now in practice in the great game of politics were not altogether unknown to our colonial forbears; inflating the voting lists and refusing to add names of those on the opposite side brought about the following petition:

"To the Magistrates of Providence:

Wee whose names are hereunto subscribed being a part of the Soulderie of the third Companey or third Traine Band in Providence humbly shewing of our greaveance unto your Honnours by way of Complaynt at our Last Election held at Roger Burllinggame Junars: in Mashantatuck on the 27th of May Last past, Severall of our Souldiers their votes were denied and the Clerk of the Band would not receive them and on the Contrari Receaved Severall vots of such as were not Souldiers of our Band and the Clerk did also deney to List several Persons that do properly belong to our band that appeared there and offered themselves and desired to be listed all which was to make a vot for themselves wee therefore do humbely pray that such disorder may be reformed So that wee may have a faire vot for our millitarie officers or else to bee placed in Sum other Company of this Towne for we cannot Submit our Selves to Traine where we are denied our Equal privilege in our voting."

It is hoped that the minority sooner or later received that consideration for which they applied.

In the annals of the town of Medford, the home of New England Rum, sobriety was the distinguishing difference between her training days and those of most other New England towns. On the fifteenth of September, 1641, begun a "muster" which lasted two days, and it was a most remarkable gathering and must have been recalled with a pardonable pride by the people of Medford for years after. There were twelve hundred soldiers present, to say nothing of the hundreds of others brought to the occasion by the peculiar attractions which this affair offered, and there was "plenty of wine and strong beer" offered for sale and doubtless drunk, as that was the day above all other days for indulging the appetite for liquors, "yet no man was drunk no oath was sworn no quarrel, no hurt done." Such a number of omissions in the history of trainings is remarkable, and we are almost led to the conclusion that it was the only such orderly affair that the town ever saw, and hence thought eminently fitting that it should be recorded.

John Dunton, the London bookseller, whose observations have been of so much value to those who write of Colonial days, describes a training at Boston, while he was there on a visit in 1685, and says: "Being come into the field the captain called us all into close order to go to prayer, and then prayed himself, and when our exercises was done the captain likewise concluded with prayer. Solemn prayer in the field upon a day of training I never knew but in New England, where it seems it is a common custom. About 3 of the clock, both our exercises and praying being over, we had a very noble dinner, to which all the clergy were invited." It is extremely doubtful if this was the custom in New England in very early times. It undoubtedly was in Boston and other parts of the Bay Colony, for all these affairs were conducted with the full Puritan form, and prayer was offered on all occasions, — at Elections, trainings, cropping of ears and boring of tongues, and even at the public execution of poor men and women for the crime of being Quakers. Under the pretence of a voluntary training at Providence, in the winter of 1655, there was a "tumult and disturbance," as the record says, involving the two political factions in that town in a bitter quarrel, which was not settled until the next summer, and then only by the solemn declaration of the town meeting that for "ye publick union & peace sake it should be past by and no more mentioned." Forgiveness was a prominent characteristic of the satellites of the great expounder of the principles of liberty, and there is a vein of humor in the serious entries upon the tattered pages of the old records of this town where this loving and forgiving spirit shines out distinct and clear. One of these acts of forgiveness or "remission of penalties," as the recording officer chose to term it, is recorded among the records of the very meeting at which the "tumult and disturbance" was so freely forgiven, and reads thus: "Whereas Henri Fowler was warned to answer for his marriage without due publication & he pleaded yt ye divisions of ye Towne were the cause of his so doing ye Towne voted a remission of his penalties." And well it might, for town boundaries were a disturbing element in this settlement for more than a century, and it has even puzzled the most astute minds to determine what these bounds were from that day to this. There is yet another entry upon these records of the forgiving kind. It was passed at a town meeting held on a training day. After the officers of the train band had been elected and certain fines for non-attendance "mitigated," the following preamble and resolution were adopted:

"Whereas Hugh Bewit complayned unto the Town Deputies against John Selden for falling on him in the night. And whereas John Selden hath Presented himself this day to the Town to give satisfaction to them for the said fact, upon his acknowledgement of the fact unto Hugh Bewit he declareth himself satisfied & upon his real submission to the town they declare themselves fully satisfied."

Submission to the majesty of the law and an apology healed the wound inflicted on Bewit.

It was directly charged against some tavern keepers, who were also captains in the militia, that they sometimes ordered trainings for the purpose of drawing a crowd around their establishments, and thereby turning the event into a merrymaking scheme for their own benefit. Captain Fenner, whose tavern was in Providence, had this charge made against him. This he resented, disputed, and finally the trouble was ventilated in a suit at law. A part of this controversy is disclosed by the following letter, written by Fenner, in which he gives the facts of a discourse on the subject on the "last of February 170¾," and says:

"I being in the Streete against Joseph Whipples talking with Major Dexter, Solomon Thornton there charged me with Severall Articules as namely upon December in the year 1703 there sum snow fell in the morning he said that the Company was not Exercised that day but only a little nere the hous sid and I said that the Company was exercised out upon the green by Lieutenant Knight he said it was not ofering to prove it saying that Richard Borden told him which he believed as soon as he would believe me and he said his brother Thomas tould him that wee had a mind to make it pase for a training day I only wanted people to cum to spend there money and I tould him that I did not want any money to be spent by him in my hous that I was willing to do the Company good I had Layd out money for them."

With all its hearsay testimony, there is enough to show that there was a suspicion among his townsmen that the training had been called for other than training purposes.

Another curious custom of training day is related as occurring in the town of Dunbarton, N. H. "At the close of the drill a hollow square was formed, into which advanced Major John Mills, then first selectman, who delivered to each man a quarter of a pound of powder, and vendued their dinner for the coming musterday to the lowest bidder, the materials for which were to be, as declared in his own words, 'good fresh beef, well baked or roasted, good wheat bread well baked; good old cider or new cider well worked.'"

In New Hampshire, it is stated, "The officers, after a short drill and a few marches and counter marches, treated liberally their men and the spectators with as much New England 'fire water' as they desired, according to the custom of the times."

There was a training at Berkeley, Mass., in the spring of 1829, at which were brought together all the military companies in Bristol county. A critical observer has left us a picture of the scenes on the training field on that occasion. Perhaps the picture is slightly overdrawn, but in the main it conveys a most excellent idea of the customs and habits at such gatherings. And what is true of this one applies equally as well to all of those old-fashioned musters of bygone days.

"There were in line, which extended for more than a mile, the yeoman guard of Bristol county — men who had worked and could fight, with locks that bent all way and untutored toes that stared each other in the face; now a white cotton hat surmounted with a red plume that looked as though it had been dipped in

'All the blood of all the Howards,'

and beside it a white one that had decked as proud, although not so distinguished, a wearer but yesterday, and that too in a similar way if we reverse the end on which it was worn.

"There were all manner of head dresses of all descriptions, old and new, great and small, from fur to felt down to wool.

"There, coats too, that had been worn from the birth day time to the eve of the American Revolution, and from that time to the present. One little scrawney dragoon in particular drew our attention, an hundred pound weight would have made him kick the beam in any honest scale and yet the pantaloons he wore would have loosely fitted a man of two hundred stone. *** The Colonel of one Regiment was the proprietor of a tent and when the duties with the Brigade would permit him, he was within the booth dealing out *Yankee military spirit* to his men. A newly elected Captain, who served under him, wished to give his men a proof of the obligation he was under to them, in advancing him to the command.

"He struck a bargain with the Colonel and advanced to the head of the company, 'Fellow Sogers' said he 'all you that belong to Captain Isaiah Gawk's company and haint had no rum nor nothin', are a gwoine to be treated to gingerbread and new cider at the Colonel's tent — please to follow arter musician Jonathan Johnson,' whereupon, the said musician Johnson stepped out of line, with an air of some consequence and, if we had seen droll ones before, they were nothing compared with him. The crown of his head was just six feet three inches and a clear from the ground and of this height, his legs constituted three fourths.

"His arms were uncommonly short and his drum was hung against his breast bone, to enable him to reach it with ease.

"A coat of red baize covered about two thirds of his back, and black gaiters ornamented his legs from the knee downward on the top of his head was a hat, it had been white, but white it was not then, nor yet black, or gray or any other color to which man had given a name. Out of the line he stepped, and out of the line was he followed by 'all those who belonged to Captain Isaiah Gawk's company and hadn't drink'd no Rum nor nothin' and as the tune 'Down thro' the bar way' rolled from his drum heads, as water rolls from a duck's back, they straggled along in a manner that showed each of them to be taking care of himself. To the tent of the Colonel they went, and in about five minutes were on the march back each with gingerbread enough in his fist to furnish a whole platoon with rations for a month."

In this brigade was the Assonet Light Infantry. The men, in this regiment, gave their commander no little uneasiness on account of "the clever way in which they would address him. Of a sudden they would gather around him for the purpose of giving him assurance of the regard which they entertained for his person. At one time we chanced to be near when they had encircled him, and when he was attempting to get them back to their places, 'Captain don't you want us to fire 'fore long.?' said a short fellow with a face like a town clock. 'Go back into line and await orders — when I want you to fire I will tell you so,' replied the commander. 'Well, Captain, when you want us to fire only let us know, and we'll fire,' and back they trudged to their posts, to remain until the spirit again moved them out."

The merry party brought thus together amused themselves at a variety of games and sports, of which fencing, running, leaping, wrestling, cudgel, stool ball, nine pins and quoits were the most popular. Over these diversions they renewed the friendships of distant friends, made new acquaintances, and drank to each other, health and prosperity, at the tavern bar.

Colonel Israel Angell of Rhode Island, on his way back from Ohio, in 1788, passed through several Connecticut towns on Training day, and he gives a brief account of what he saw and incidentally refers to the overcrowded condition of the tavern at which he had proposed to put up, and he writes, under the date of October 6, "went to Wallingford (Conn.) to one Captain Carringtons here was 3 or 4 Companeys of Militia horse & foot as it was a General Training day throughout the State. Saw the troops assembled in every place through which I passed the tavern was full here however Captain Carrington said my hors should be well taken care of & I should have lodgings at one of his neighbors a few rods from his Door."

Important notices, royal proclamations and other information for the consideration of the townsmen were given on training day, at the head of the military there assembled. A wider distribution of such information was insured, for every one was on hand, as it was the day of all days for the interchange of news, gossip and opinions.

Upon the death of King Charles the Second, and the accession of James the Second to the throne, due proclamation was made throughout New England. The reading of such a notice was a momentous event, and the formalities attending it are well described in the records of the town of Providence, for they were written by the man chosen to read this important notice and perform the ceremony, Thomas Olney, the town clerk. No doubt his bosom swelled with pride when he read the royal document and when he recorded these words:

"Whereas the towne of Providence hath received an order from their Governor & Councill bearing date the 24th day of April 1685 informing that their said Governor hath received a letter from ye Honorable Lords of ye prive Councill bearing date White Hall the sixth day of February 168I Informing of ye decease of our late dred Sovereign King Charles the Second. And the Proclamation of his Royal Highness James Duke of Yorke & Albany his said Majestyes Only Brother Our only lawfull Lineall & Rightfull Liege Lord James the Second by the Grace of God King of England Scotland ffrance & Ireland Defender of the faith &c. In said letter also requireing the said Proclamation to be made & Sollemnized in this his Majestyes Collony of Rhode Island & Providence Plantations. In which said Order the said Govenor & Councill ordered ye same Proclamation to be made at ye towne of Providence on ffriday the first of May following & Read by such person as should by ye Assistants in said Town be appointed.

"In obedience whereunto the Assistants of said town appoynted the towne Clarke open and publicly to Read the said Proclamation in the head of the Traine Band in three publike places of the Towne. The which was duly attended unto & Solemnly performed upon Friday the first day of May 1685 in the head of the Traine Band there together in military Order & in presence of ye assistants & principle inhabitants of said Towne."

In the territory now covered by the state of Maine, and which was a part of the Massachusetts Colony, it was the custom to inflict punishment upon offenders, on the training day before the militia drawn up in order. At Kennebunk, it is recorded, that the culprit was sentenced to be taken to the training field and there "at the head of a military company to have twenty-five stripes on his naked back and have his neck and heels tied together for a full hour," a performance which must have been a striking object lesson to many in the assembly. In the town of Kittery, in 1670, another form of punishment was brought into requisition, and an unfortunate fellow "road the woodin Horse for dangerous and churtonous caridge to his commander and mallplying of oaths."

There is much else about training day that is best forgotten. As a moral influence it was not a success, while the cause of temperance was not greatly advanced by the custom. It was destined to remain one of the permanent institutions of town life, and although it underwent many changes, it was not until within comparatively recent years that it ceased altogether. The musters or trainings of later days were not unlike the Train Band days of colonial times, except they were on a more elaborate scale, both in attendance and dissipation. The gew-gaws and paraphernalia of the muster have given way to the more orderly and better disciplined encampment of the National Guard. The old training field, so jealously guarded from encroachment by our ancestors, no longer receives the tread of martial feet. The streets and lanes about it are no longer covered with tents and shelters where gingerbread, small beer, and "beer of a larger brew," apples, cider, nuts and buns were offered for sale. The echoes of the fife and drum which awakened such thrills of excitement and enthusiasm have faded away, and those brown-visaged country youths, arrayed in showy uniforms and glittering accoutrements, with breasts bursting with pride, patriotism and cotton wadding, have broken ranks and the muster is ended.

Chapter Five - Tavern Cheer and Charge

THE great room or main room of the tavern was the most important part of the establishment.

Here was the cavernous fireplace, taking up nearly the entire end of the room, and in which, during the cold winter season, huge logs crackled and blazed, sending showers of sparks up the great chimney stack into the sharp, crisp air. In the summer time it was often filled with green shrubs or logs piled neatly upon the fire dogs or andirons. The floor, of hard oak boards, was sanded and was kept white and smooth by the proverbially neat colonial housewife. John Dunton describes her as she appeared to him at the inn at Ipswich. "Mrs. Steward," he says, "is of a middle size, her face round and pretty, her speech and behavior gentle and courteous. She is all obedience; the hyacinth follows not the sun more willingly than she her husband's pleasure. Her household is her charge; her only pride is to be neat and cleanly. She is both wise and religious, and, in a word, whatsoever men may talk of magick, there none charms like her." And he is also as clear in his description of the landlord, for he says: "He is so kind a husband he is worthy of the wife he enjoys, and would even make a bad wife good by example."

Scattered about the room were chests, chairs, forms, settles and stools. The room was low studded, with great beams running across overhead. The bar, the main attraction of the room, was usually in a corner. Sometimes a sort of wooden portcullis, which could be raised or lowered at pleasure, served this purpose, while in other cases a "buffet" built into the corner furnished this important adjunct to the great room.

There was another indispensable article of the great room furnishings, and it always stood or hung by the fireplace, and at the "Elm Tree Inn" at Farmington it is there to-day. This was the flip iron, which was used so often in the concoction of certain beverages. It had other curious names, for Mrs. Earle, in the "*Customs and Habits in Colonial New England*," tells us it was sometimes called the "loggerhead, hottle or flip dog." This, when heated and thrust into the liquor, gave to it a peculiar bitter flavor, which was dearly loved by those who enjoyed such drinks. Sometimes this instrument became worn and broken from frequent heatings and other causes, and had to be turned over to the skillful hand of the village blacksmith for repairs. Such an occurrence took place at Bowen's tavern at Barrington, and on the old daybook formerly kept by him is this entry:

"Josiah Viall, Cr.
For mending flip iron, 8d."

And he took his pay in trade, for on the day when this charge was made, December 27, 1775, he had "1 gill of West India Rum at 4d," and two days later another gill, and thus squared the account.

The testimony is conflicting as to the quality of New England inns, but the patronage which they all seem to have enjoyed is some evidence of their popularity. This popularity, too, was based on different qualifications. May's tavern, at Canton, Mass., and Danforth's tavern, at Cambridge, were celebrated for their concoctions of flip; Brigham's tavern, at Westborough, for "mulled wine," which is said to have been made according to the following recipe: "One-quart Madeira, boiling hot, one half pint hot water, six eggs, beaten light: sugar to taste." Another tavern, on Cape Cod, was noted for the excellence of its pumpkin pies. Henry Bowen seems to have derived much popularity from his punch, which he prepared in a "Large Defiance punch bowl." He also served his patrons with flip and battered flip, which he sold for nine pence a mug, or four- and one-half pence a half mug. This was made of beer, a beaten egg stirred up with it, then stirred with the red hot flip iron, loggerhead, or whatever the instrument may have been called, and finally, just before serving, a dash of rum was poured in.

A list of drinks popular in New England contains the following: "punch, cider, strong beer, porter, grog, madeira, port, sherry toddy, claret, sangaree and toddy." But there were many others of as general popularity as these, for there was rum, both New England and West Indie, brandy, "sillebub," "Jonava" (Gin), metheglin, sack mum, ale, and no end of mixtures of which these formed the base. When Sir Edmund Andros came into power in New England, he levied a tax or duty on all liquors brought into the colonies, and those named in the act providing for this excise were "Fayal wines or any other wines of the Western Islands, Madeira, Malaga, Canary, Tent and Alicant."

Cider was the most common drink of the colonists, for it was not long before the scions from Mr. Blackstone's orchard bore "fare fruite," and cider mills, cider presses and cider troughs were in most of the townsmen's possession, while cider was listed in nearly every inventory of an estate. It was served in many forms, egg cider, which was "9d a mug," "cyder 2d a pot," and mulled cider, cider royal, and cider famed. An early traveller in New England says: "At the tap room in Boston I have had an ale quart of cider spiced and sweetened with sugar for a groat," equivalent to four pence. As orchards increased and the fruit became more plenty, this commodity became cheaper, and in the early part of the eighteenth century was sold for three shillings a barrel, but in 1760 it was six and seven shillings for the same quantity. Its price was influenced largely by the apple crop, for there were "off years" in colonial days just as in modern times. John Houghton, of Lancaster, who kept tavern for many years, sent the following letter to the Middlesex County Court in Massachusetts, in 1715, and he bewails the scarcity of cider in that year.

To Capt. Samuel Phipps of Charlestown.

Worthy Sr: — After my Humble Service & Due Respects Presented to ye Hon'r'able Justices of ye County of Middlesex together with yourselfe, these are to acquaint you that I am under such Indisposition of Body that I could not attend this Last Session of ye General Assembly, nor can I as yet Possibly (with comfort) come to pay my excise nor to Renew my License, but I have sent ye money for ye last years excise by Joseph Brabrook the Bearer hereof, which I hope will be to acceptance & in case yor Honrs shall see cause that my Licence may be continued.

I hope you will abate neer one half of ye excise for Doubtless I have paid very Deare considering what I have Drawne compared with other Townes. I had but one Hogshead of Rum ye last yeare & that wanted about 12 Gallons of being full when I bought it & it wants severall Gallons of being out now besides aboute 10 or 12 Gallons Lent out & were it not that I am concerned with writing of Deeds & Bonds & other Public Concerns of ye Townes affaires, which Occasion Persons often to come to my House, in order to signing & Issuing such things, I should not be willing to be concerned with a Licence; for what Drinks I sell I do it as cheap as at Boston & besides ye first cost I pay twenty shillings per Hogshead for carrying it up, besides the Hazard, & as for Cyder there is none to be had nor like to be this yeare at any price fruit is so scarce & for wine I never sold 5 Gallons in all ye years I have had a licence. So that my Draught being so Little (there being no road or thoroughfare for travelers through our towne) I hope your Hon. will consider ye Premises & do therein as in your Wisdom and Justice it shall seem meet which will oblige

Your Humble Servant
John Houghton.
Dat Lan' July ye 27 1715.

Some years later this condition was reversed, for in the old account book of Judge Joseph Wilder of this town there is "an account of cyder made in the year 1728," which was distributed among the townspeople in the following quantities:

	Barrels.
"for the Reverend Mr. John Prentice	61
" Capt Samuel Willard	12½
" Benjamin Wilson	52
" Thomas Wilder	22½
" Jos Wilder	17
" William Divol	5
" John Divol	15
" Jonas Houghton	6
" Jos Wheelock	21
" Joshua Houghton	63
" Ebenz Wilder	47½
" James Houghton	5
" Chas Sawyer	9½
" Richard Wild	9
" Jonathan Houghton	16
" Ebenezer Prescott	31
" Daniel Rugg	20½
" James Wilder	39
" William Houghton	113
" William Sawyer	23
" James Butler	17½
" Widow Rugg	7½
" Philip Larkin	2½
	———
	616 "

Cider making was an important industry in Lancaster, and was taken into consideration when the town undertook to lay out its highways. In the year 1734 the proprietors of the Nichewaug lands agreed with Captain Jonas Houghton, surveyor, to build a road "from Lancaster along the north side of Wachusett." In this agreement it was stipulated that this highway should not be accepted unless it be "so feasible...as to carry comfortably, with four oxen four barrels of cider at once."

Sillabub was another mixture which appears to have been more or less popular; it cost four pence a pot. The method of preparing it is thus described:

"Fill your sillabub Pot with cyder (for that is best for a Sillabub) and a good store of sugar put in as much thick cream by two or three spoonsful at a time, as hard as you can, as though you milk it in then stir it together exceeding softly over and about and let it stand two hours at least."

Another recipe is as follows:

"Take the juice and grated outer skyne of a large Lemon four glasses of cyder a quarter of a pound of syfted sugar mix the above and let it stand some hours, then whip it & add a pint of thick cream and the whites of two Eggs cut to a froth."

Home brewed beer had some users but it was not so often called for as cider and liquors of a "stronger size."

Our colonial forbears seem to have preferred a more fiery mixture for the full gratification of their taste.

Major Thomas Fenner of Neutaconconet, made great quantities of beer which he doubtless disposed of, for there are charges of it by the barrel at 3 shillings a barrel, and here is his recipe for making it:

"Receipt to make Bear

One ounce of Sentry Suckery or Sulindine one handful Red Sage or Large ¼ Pound Shells of Iron Brused fine take 10 quarts of Water Steep it away to Seven and a quart of Molases Wheat Brand Baked Hard one quart of Malt one handfull Sweeat Balm. Take it as Soone as it is worked."

"Beer of the best kind" was sold at Salem in 1670 for 1½d a quart. Rum undiluted is the most common among tavern charges, while grog by the "Bole," "dobel bole," or nip, stands a close second. An old account book contains, among a number of similar entries, "Oct the 25 1706 then Reconed with John Absalom and all accounts balanced then due to balance:

" More money lent him	oo	5	6
More one jile of Rum			3
More half a pint			6
More for Rum			7
More money		oɪ	oɪ
for cyder			o2
for cyder			o2
More for Rum			o6
for Rum & cyder		oɪ	
for Rum and cyder			o6 "

In the days before court houses, town houses and other buildings for the transaction of public business, the tavern was utilized for all such purposes, and the records of the ancient towns and counties contain the accounts which the freemen were called upon to pay for the expenses of their public officers at such places.

While there is no great complaint of extravagance, or examples of the abuse of this privilege or custom on the part of officials in their dealings with the tavern keepers, it was thought advisable by the magistrates of Cambridge that some regulations be adopted relative to the tavern charges for the County Court, and in December, 1679, it was stipulated that henceforth for the jurors there shall be allowed in money:

" For their breakfast one man			o o 4	
For their dinner	"	"	o 1 3	
For their supper	"	"	o 1 o"	

For the magistrates:

For dinner one man		o 2 o	
For supper	" "	o 1 6	

For the marshal and constable:

A meal	o 1 o"

As it is unlikely that there was any difference in the quality or quantity of the food furnished either class of public servants, the greater sum allowed the magistrates and officers of the court was probably for liquid refreshments.

The selectmen of Cambridge, however, do not seem to have been restricted in their allowances, and they dined and wined at the public expense at the "Blue Anchor Tavern," in which Governor Jonathan Belcher was born.

In 1749, and for many years thereafter, this tavern was conducted by Ebenezer Bradish, and his charges for the entertainment of the selectmen are found in the following bill:

"The Selectmen of the town of Cambridge

				To Ebenezer Bradish Dr		
March	1769	To dinners and drink		0	17	8
April	"	To flip and punch		0	2	0
May	"	To wine and eating		0	6	8
May	1769	To dinners drink and suppers		0	18	0
	"	To flip and cheese		0	1	8
	"	To wine and flip		0	4	0
June	"	To punch		0	2	8
July	"	To punch and eating		0	4	0
August	"	To punch and cheese		0	3	7
Oct	"	To punch and flip		0	4	8
	"	To dinners and drink		0	13	8
Due Jan 1770 & Feb		Sundries		0	12	0
				4	10	7 "

A bill of the town council of Bristol, (R. I.), for entertainment furnished at Stephen Wardwell's tavern during the year 1795, amounted to £12-3-2, and was made up of so many items that it is a monotonous repetition of "nips of grog," "Dubel boles of tod," "Brandi sling," punch and rum, with occasional charges for "Supers."

The town council of Providence, in 1784, usually assembled at Esek Aldrich's tavern and his charges read as follows:

"To the use of my house at ten diff'rnt times on business of the Town having furnished one double Bowie of punch & two Bottle of wine 3-12-0." Another bill reads: "To House Room Fire and Bottle of wine 9s." Another has charged: "To Room Wine Candle & Fire &c 0-12-0." While yet another: "To Room Wine Fire Candles &c 0-15-0," the "&c" doubtless accounting for the variation in prices.

Ames' tavern at Dedham was a popular place for dinner parties, and this letter will convey some idea of what was provided for the guests on such occasions.

There is no mention of any liquors, but it is safe to say that they were not omitted at table, even if they were from the bill of fare proposed.

"Before I heard from you this morning the Gentlemen had concluded to dine at Gay's but I took the pains to see 'em again & we have agreed to have the Dinner at your house. I hope you will have every thing in that agreeable & genteel order that will Recommend your house to the Gentlemen & my preference of it before Gays acceptable to them & the Ladys

I am your able Servant,
Ezekiel Price.

We propose Bacon
   Lamb
   Chicken
   Green Peas &ctr Asparagrass
   Sauces &ctr for the Dinner.

There will be about twelve chaises including those we meet so that you will provide for 24 persons.

We are to meet some Company from Newport who will set out tomorrow & the next day being Wednesday we shall set out & be at your house abt 10 "Clock unless the Weather is so bad we can't proceed.

Monday morning June 11 1753."

In the town of Medford the rate of charges at the taverns were fixed as follows:

"West India toddy one bowl	18s
" " flipp one mug	18s
New England Toddy per bowl	12s
New England flip a mug	12s
Breakfast	18s
Common meat supper	20s"

When the courts met at the taverns, they became the resort of large numbers of people, attracted thereto by the nature of the proceedings. Some of the culprits were neighbors and some of the crimes or misdemeanors had been the subject of household discussion for weeks and months. The whole neighborhood was deeply interested or morbid curiosity greatly aroused so that a large crowd always put in an appearance, much to the gratification of the tavern keeper, who was to be the most benefitted by the proceedings. In what is now York county, in Maine, the courts were usually held at the tavern of Samuel Austin. The jurors who were in attendance at the trials were allowed "two meals a day at the expense of the county," which, considering the great distance that many of them had to travel when responding to the summons of the sheriff was not a very liberal allowance. Viewed in the light of modern methods for conducting such proceedings, the manner in which the courts were opened at Austin's tavern is worth mentioning. At the hour appointed, the court drummer, an important functionary, took up his station at the tavern door and beat the drum; for this service he was allowed two shillings a day, twice what a juror received for patiently listening to these long stories of crime and misconduct. This tattoo on the drum was the signal for the populace to draw near and give their attendance. The county court held its session at Austin's tavern in Wells, during a whole week in July, 1670, and the bill which landlord Austin presented, for the expense of this session, was made up of these items:

"Magistrates and jurors   37 07 07
John Bennett expenses of John Potter the murderer   16 0
John Smith the drummer for 6 days attendance   12 0"

A curious lot of cases were determined in this Court at different times. In 1661 John Roadman was presented for saying "he belonged to the Divil, and if the Divil had his due he had had him seven years ago." In 1668 Rowland Hansell was presented "for living in this Country six or seven years, he having a wife in England," while several more or less good townsmen and their wives were all brought before the Court for "profane speech," it being alleged that they commonly used, as an answer to questions propounded, the words, "the Divil a bit;" and they punished some of these offenders, too, in a m.ost thorough manner, for in 1661 George Gaylord was subjected to thirty-nine lashes "for visiting the widow Hitchcock."

Other irregularities and misdemeanors were punished with a fine, and to illustrate the scale of prices for certain breaches of the law, this curious record is given. It is found in the town of Westborough, Mass.

"A fine paid by Benj Warren for uttering Two profane Oaths   0 5 0
"A fine paid by Joseph Rice, Jr., of Northborough, for uttering three profane oaths and two profane curses   0 8 0
"A fine paid by William Nus in Westborough for uttering two Profane Curses
                                                                                                                0 6 0"

Profane curses cost three shillings each, while profane oaths were less expensive. In the heat of passion, or in animated discussion, it must have taken much skill to formulate a sufficiently expressive retort consistent with economy.

The attractions of the tavern at Cambridge were more than the students at Harvard College could resist, the students of 1672 being not unlike those of to-day. So frequently were they found within its doors, and so loth was landlord Gibson to dispense with their custom and company, that at last, as a means of correcting the habits of the young men and checking this irregularity of the landlord, he was waited upon by the constables of the town for "entertaining some of the students contrary to law," and on October 1, 1672, having been convicted of this offence, he was sentenced "to be admonished and to pay a fine of forty shillings in money," and stand committed until it was paid.

It was only at the tavern that opportunity was offered for social gatherings for the amusement of young and old, and in the eighteenth century the strict rules previously in force regulating the conduct of such places had been materially modified. The various tavern keepers made ample provision for the wants of the people, and provided means for the entertainment of those who resorted to their ho uses. Benjamin Parker, the town treasurer of Medford, when he built his commodious establishment, in 1745, provided a large dance hall, which supplied at once a long felt want. Dancing at taverns had been common enough even in the early days of the New England towns. So common, in fact, that in 1631 the Massachusetts Bay authorities, in "consequence of some miscarriages at weddings" which had taken place at the taverns, passed a law prohibiting dancing on such occasions at public houses.

But in 1745 orderly assemblages for the purpose of dancing and its incidental sociability were not regarded with disfavor. These old time dances which brightened for a moment the dull life of the period would not awaken much enthusiasm in the hearts of the youth of to-day. But to those brown-faced, stalwart country youths, and those red-cheeked, hearty colonial maidens, they were the height of pleasure and enjoyment.

The music supplied on such occasions was the flute, viol, or spinnet. The minuet, the most graceful and artistic of all the dances of Colonial days, was probably seldom witnessed on the floors of Parker's tavern, but the old-time contra dances, where the first gentleman was "to foot it to the second lady and both turn single," and the "first three couples haze, then lead down in the middle and back again," where "the first couple three hands round with the second lady, allemand; three hands round with the second gentleman, allemand again; lead down two couples, up again, cast off one couple, hands round with the third, right hand and left," were gone through with all the spirit and enthusiasm of enjoyment. Then, after refreshing with the good things to eat, which had been bountifully provided in the great dining room, it made an evening the recollection of which lived in the minds of those boys and girls of the farms for months afterwards, and was even recalled in after life over and over again.

The law, too, with respect to "bowls, quoits, loggets, ninepins and billiards," had been "mitigated," and another Medford tavern keeper built a bowling-alley in his house, and thereby added to the vocabulary of the good people of the town such words as "strikes" and "spares."

No better place for the exhibition of strange animals and other novelties could be found than at the tavern. The tavern keeper, when such opportunities offered, was ready and willing to give up a part of his stables or other outbuildings for such purposes. It drew a crowd and benefitted him as much as it did the showman, for all these "curiosities" were freely discussed before the tavern bar; after they had been examined by those attracted to the show. A Polar bear is not now regarded as a "monstrous sight," but the following advertisement, printed in the *Columbian Sentinel*, shows how such an animal was looked upon in 1810.

"MONSTROUS SIGHT.

To be seen at A. Pollard's Tavern, Elm Street. A White Greenland Sea Bear, which was taken at Sea weighing 1000 wt. They have been seen several leagues at sea, and sometimes floating on cakes of ice.

This animal displays a great natural curiosity.

Admittance 12 1-2 cts.

Children half Price."

Another natural curiosity was advertised in this wise:

"A beautiful MOOSE.

The Curious in Natural History are invited to Major King's Tavern, where is to be seen a fine young MOOSE of sixteen hands in height, and well proportioned. The properties of this fleet and tractable Animal are such as will give pleasure and satisfaction to every beholder.
Price of Admission, Nine Pence."

Near this same establishment there was exhibited "a beautiful African Lion," notice of which was published in the *Boston Gazette*, Aug. 13, 1801, in the following attractive manner:
"To the Curious.
A beautiful African LION
To be seen every day in the week (Sundays excepted) in *Brattle-street*, next to Major King's near the Market, where a very convenient situation is provided for those Ladies and Gentlemen who may please to favor the proprietor with their presence.
THIS noble Animal is between three and four feet high, measures eight feet from nostrils to tail, and a beautiful dun color; 11 years old, and weighs near 500 wt. — His legs and tail are as thick as those of a common size ox. He was caught in the woods of Goree, in Africa, when a whelp; and brought from thence to New York. Great attention has been paid in providing a strong substantial Cage, and to have the Lion under very good command. The person who has the care of him can comb his mane, make him lie down and get up at any time: and it is said by those who have seen Lions in the Tower of London, and many parts that he is really worth the contemplation of the curious.
Admittance 25 cents. — Children half price."
Market day was another happy time for the tavern keepers, but they could not have grown rich on the prices paid for "bed and dyet," for all this, and even more, could be had for three shillings a day. It was the extras, the sales at the bar, that made the day a notable one in tavern life.

The taverns at Medford are said to have been filled every night during the winter with New Hampshire and Vermont farmers, who had come to town, bringing with them butter, pork, grass seed, poultry and other farm products, to dispose of on market days. These occasions were regulated by town laws, and places were designated where the market should be kept. At Providence they were set up near the taverns, at Olney's and at Whipple's. A town officer, called the Clerk of the Market, regulated the conduct of these places. In the city of Providence this officer is now regularly elected each year.

A story is told of one of these New Hampshire farmers, who, while on his way to market, put up over night at a tavern a few miles out of Boston. That evening a party of young people came to the inn for a dance and a general good time. During the evening, while they were enjoying themselves, the old farmer became interested in the actions of this gay company, and as such affairs were none too common in his life, the novelty of it prompted him to go down stairs, and without any feeling that he was intruding, he took up a position near a window and watched the proceedings with eager eyes. One of the company, observing him, and having, doubtless, imbibed too freely of the liquors with which the party was supplied, took from the table a decanter and threw it at his head. The window and the decanter were both broken, and the face of the surprised farmer slightly injured. Such a good shot aroused much enthusiasm among the party, and the thrower was cheered and congratulated, all agreeing that it was a good joke on the farmer. But the injured man did not so regard it. He retired from the spot, and with a mental resolve that he would be even with them, returned to his room. Here he dressed his wounds, and then descended to the yard and straightway made for the stable, where he sought out each vehicle in which the party had arrived, took out the linch-pins and hid them.

Then he retired to his room and was soon sleeping. At a late hour the dancers departed, filled with merriment and other things of which there had been a store. The details of the collapse which followed their departure have not been preserved. But it is said that the old gentleman, saw enough on the roadside next morning to show him that he had been successful, and that his injuries had been avenged.

It was a busy day at the tavern when the auction, the notice of which had been displayed about the tavern for weeks, took place, for these usually occurred at the tavern; especially was this so when personal belongings were to be sold, and human beings also. Human beings of two classes were sold at the taverns, criminals and paupers. At Israel Clifford's tavern in Dunbarton, N. H., one Gould, a sheep thief, was sold at public auction for "damages and costs," taxed at £2-12-10; previous to this sale he was "whipped thirteen stripes by Archibald Stark Constable."

One of the townsmen bid off the culprit and he was set at work to break and clean flax.

He applied himself to this labor with such success that after he had dressed as much as he could carry he departed for parts unknown, very much to the grief of his purchaser.

But there is a more pathetic side to these tavern auctions of human beings, for it was customary in some New England towns to dispose of the town's poor in this way. In the town of Wareham, on Buzzard's Bay, at the tavern of Benjamin Fearing, such events frequently took place. "The sales were made," says Bliss in his *Colonial Times on Buzzard's Bay*, "in the bar room of the inn, where the landlord as he served the thirsty guests from his decanters, discussed with them the value of the services of the paupers, for whose keeping they had come to bid," and the town records bear silent testimony to these sad phases of colonial life in the following words:

"Jurned from the meeting house down to Benjamin Fearings house to van-due the poor."

In contradistinction to this sad side of tavern life, is the event which took place at the Saugus tavern in 1756. It is a most curious happening and its like was seldom witnessed, for it was an encounter between two men eminent in the neighborhood for their wit and humor, and resolved itself into a sort of duel with ideas instead of the more deadly weapons commonly used.

These two individuals were Jonathan Gowen of Lynn and Joseph Emerson of Reading. At the appointed time for this exhibition of humorous gymnastics, the tavern was filled with a merry, rollicking crowd, cheering and encouraging the two champions to their best efforts. So great was the crowd that all the space inside the doors was taken up, and that none should be deprived of all this display of sparkling wit, an adjournment was taken to an open field near the house, where these Yankee humorists could have full play and the crowd full hearing.

What kind of a performance this resulted in or what kind of buffoonery took place, contemporary annalists have neglected to perpetuate, but when this "fight" was over the Reading wit was vanquished. How this was determined has not been handed down to posterity, but it has been recorded that Gowen's wit "was beyond all human imagination." But, alas, he was destined to fall from the dizzy height to which he had been elevated by this strange exhibition, for he gradually lost his bright mind, his wit faded, and he ceased at length to be even funny, and finally became so stupid that the expression, "you are as dull as Jonathan Gowen," became proverbial. There were other exhibitions about the tavern which inured to the benefit of the tavern keeper and the townsmen too, for that matter, but not to all.

The stocks and the whipping post were near neighbors of the tavern, and whenever the courts had decreed that an offender should be punished there was always a crowd about the place. These appliances for the administration of justice were of different forms; at some places regularly built stocks were set up, as at David Arnold's tavern in Warwick, R. I., where "John Lowe was ordered to erect the public stocks and whipping post near David Arnold's tavern, and to procure iron and timber for the same;" a similar order provided for their erection near the tavern of Thomas Angell, in Scituate, R.I. The stocks were not elaborately constructed, but consisted of a frame built a few feet from the ground, and whereon was placed two sticks of timber between which the legs of the culprit were confined. The whipping post was less elaborate in construction; most anything that was substantial enough to stand the writhings and strainings given by the unfortunate person who was tied to it, was sufficient for the purpose. Sometimes a tree standing conveniently near by was utilized for this purpose, as at the old Gavitt tavern in Westerly, R. I., and this old oak, as bereft of foliage as a stalk of asparagus, yet full of life, stands there to-day, looking as though it was doing penance for the many cruelties there from time to time inflicted. But it was not always essential that the regular whipping post be used on such occasions, for poor Lydia

Wardwell, wrought up to the highest pitch of religious frenzy, for walking into the meeting house at Ipswich, naked, "was taken thence and tyed to the fence post of the tavern," and sorely lashed while the hard-hearted Puritan townspeople looked on and saw this horrible treatment inflicted upon "a young and tender chaste woman." That grewsome structure, the gallows, too, was a companion of the tavern, and in the town of Cambridge stood near Porter's tavern. This fact seems to have inspired some ancient rhymster to inscribe the following:

"Cambridge is a famous town,
    Both for wit and knowledge,
  Some they whip and some they hang.
    And some they send to college."

Execution day at Cambridge was an event of great interest to the people of this town, and neighboring towns as well. From the diary of a Boston man we get some idea of the way he spent the day, and thus judge how the day was passed by others, for he writes:

"Thursday the 18th day of Septr (1755)

Execution day a clear but for the time of year a Cold day about 1 o'clock sat out for Cambridge saw ye execution Mark hanged and Phillis burnt then to Bradishes, & then to morses drank some punch with Mr Moreley Tom Leverett Mr Cooper Tom foxcroft Ned Emerson & others & walked down with Jonathan Bradish and then to mr Moreleys house tarried till ten supped & refreshed nature and then went home sufficiently and went to bed & slept woke up very finely refreshed."

Execution day, with its writhing, hanging forms and the odor of burnt flesh, seems to have acted on him as a mild tonic. It was also a gala day at Bradish's tavern, and punch and other mixtures flowed freely down the parched throats of the multitude that had assembled to hear "Mr. Appleton preach to the people, but more especially to the prisoners who were to die, from Proverbs ye 13th, at the 15th verse: 'The Way of the Transgressor is Hard'" and then witness the proceedings when they were launched into eternity. Altogether there was a certain cheerfulness about the occasion, and it was doubtless looked upon as a day of hand shaking, merry making and deep drinking.

Madam Knight, that early inter-colonial traveller, on her journey from Boston to New York, in 1704, stopped for a time at Ames' Tavern, in Dedham, to procure a guide. In her diary of her journeyings she mentions visiting at this time the Rev. Joseph Belcher, the minister of that town. After the Revolution, this house being conducted by a Mrs. Woodward, was known as Woodward's Tavern, at the sign of the "Law Book."

It is related that the tap room windows were screened with heavy wooden shutters, in which were small heart shaped openings. In the evening, when this room was lighted, these little openings emitted a brilliant streak of light, and travellers as they passed along the highway, or in crossing the meadows, seeing the light in the darkness, were wont to remark to each other, "See the light shine through Mrs. Woodward's heart."

Near the bar, or in a convenient quarter of the main room in most of the taverns, was a desk, usually nothing more than a box with a slanting lid, which could be raised at will. On this stood an ink horn, a sand box and quill box. Inside this desk or on the top of it, there was always kept the tavern account book, wherein were recorded the various transactions which the landlord had with his customers. Here were carefully registered the pints and quarts which the bibulous townsmen had charged up against them. Many of these curious old books are yet preserved, and they form the outline for a most complete series of sketches of the every day life of the people and complete pictures of life at the tavern. They are of all sizes, shapes and conditions, from a few leaves of irregularly shaped paper stitched together, to substantially bound volumes in vellum; but whatever their form, the entries upon their now torn and finger-marked pages are pretty much of the same character. Let us examine one and dwell for a time on the life in Barrington more than a hundred years ago, as reflected by the old day book of Squire Bowen, erstwhile tavern keeper and store keeper in that section of the Massachusetts colony since transferred to Rhode Island. Like many other taverners he kept the country store, and he dealt in all sorts of commodities, horn combs, "scains of fine thread," gingerbread, almanacks, cord wood, coffins, and New England rum by the hogshead. The country store as it existed in colonial days has disappeared from modern life, but now and then in some remote country town there may be found one that has not lost entirely its old time characteristics. There is one to-day in a little New England town, which has masqueraded for years under the metropolitan title of Hopkinton City, where the people of the village congregate at evening and exchange the news and gossip of the place, where politics are discussed, and politics here are politics, for three governors have been selected from this little village and two have come from this store; crops, too, are prophesied, and so are all manner of subjects, just as the ancestors of those who assemble there today talked and prophesied more than a hundred years before.

The villagers, too, buy their household supplies at the same counter that their fathers, grandfathers, and great grandfathers leaned up against and counted out their money. The room is low studded and dingy, for the little windows, shaded by the shelving, admit but little light. A counter, now scratched and splintered with a century's trade, extends across the room with a slight sweep inward. Behind the counter, shelves fill up the space not taken up by the little windows, whereon are displayed every conceivable article for household use. In front of the counter and in the middle of the store there used to stand an old-fashioned iron box stove, or, as they were sometimes called, a wood burner. It was one of the first enclosed stoves ever built, and until within a few years has regularly performed its winter service. Now its place is filled with a modern coal burner, and this old relic has been carefully set away.

Opening from the store are three doors, one into the dwelling house, which adjoins the store, another into a little room wherein is stored the more bulky commodities like molasses, vinegar, oil and such articles, and I suspect that, in the days long ago, hogsheads of rum might have been found here, but not now. Another door, one of those curious Dutch doors with shutters, opens out to the village street.

Above the store is the loft, where the extra stock is kept, and there are to-day stored away in this little space articles purchased for the shop more than seventy years ago. The collector of old china would here find a rich store on which to feast his eyes; but it would end there, for these old treasures are highly prized by the owner, and no consideration would tempt him to part with them. Hanging at one end of the counter from the side of the shelving there is a string of button moulds, just where it has hung for forty years.

Perhaps Henry Bowen's store was like this, but if not, it is too late now to tell, for his old shop was destroyed by fire some years since. Let us assume that it was, and enter and live for a brief time with his friends and neighbors. Beside the open window Squire Bowen sits sleeping in his chair. The air is redolent with the perfume of jessamine and flowering currant and the hum of dozens of bumble bees, the only sound to be heard, is not sufficient to awake him, while we tip-toe to the desk and scan the pages of his old day book, lying open as he left it before dropping off into sleep.

'Tis haying time and many of his neighbors have been obliged to purchase the necessary appliances for cutting the rich meadow grass, and the charges read:

" Thomas Allin   Dr

To 1 scythe   5—

Capt. Aaron Barney of Rehoboth   Dr

To 1 scythe   5—6
To 1 sickle   1—4

Esther Tiffany   Dr

To 1 scythe Dld yr Negro Danl.   5—6 "

Perhaps if they had not left the old one hanging in the crotch of the apple trees to rust through the winter, they would not have been called upon to make this outlay.

But there have been other customers, doubtless returning from or going to the hay field, as these items seem to show:

" Consider Tripp   Dr

To ½ Gil Bitters   2d

Joshua Bicknell   Dr

To 1 Gil W. Rum   4d
To ½ bowl Toddy   5d

Thomas Allin   Dr

To 2 bowls Punch @ 1s 4d   2s   8d
To 1 mess oats for Doct Bradfords
  hors   3d

John Rogers Richmond   Dr

To 1 qt N. Rum dld yr indian boy   7½d

Josiah Viall   Dr

To 1 pt Jamaica Spirits   8d "

Josiah Viall was the blacksmith and he shod the store keeper's horse:

" Josiah Viall   Cr

By setting my horses shoes behind   8d
By setting & steeling my horses
  hind shoes   10d "

He also mended the flip iron and generally took his pay in liquor, for the next charge, but one after the above is

" Josiah Viall   Dr

To 1 Pt Jamaica Spirits   7¼d "

and the next day

" Josiah Viall   Dr

To 2 Qts Jamaica Spirits   2s   3d "

thus overdrawing his account.

Joshua Bicknell was a frequent customer at the tavern and store, and he seems to have been the most unfortunate of all of Bowen's customers, and these charges against him appear upon this open book:

" Joshua Bicknell Esq   Dr

To cash paid Mr. Chaffee for mending my cart ladder irons which you
  broke   3s
To 1 iron hoop you lost off my cart
  exaltree   1s
To 1 stake bar you broke   1s "

And a few days later more trouble for goodman Bicknell is indicated in this entry:

> " To cash paid Natt Heath for
> making one cart ladder which
> you broke   6s "

And then again:

> " Joshua Bicknell   Dr
> To ½ Gil W Rum   2d
> To 1 qt W Rum   1s   1d
> To 1 wine glass you broke   9d "

His dealings with Bowen, seem to have resulted in a general breaking up of everything he laid his hands on. But he was not the only unfortunate person who damaged the property of the Squire, for there appears to have been another, and the charge for this breakage reads thus:

> " Samuel Allen 2d Esq
> To breaking my arm'd chair   3   0
> To breaking one Square of glass
> in my window   7
> To splitting of the groove of a
> panel door   2   0
>   ———
>   5   7 "

It would be interesting to know if there is any connection between this charge and the following, which are found registered at about the same time:

> " Samuel Allen 2d Esq
> TO 1½ mugs flip @ 9d   1   1½
> To 1 bowl toddy   9 "

> " Samuel Allen 2d Esq
> To ½ Gil Bitters   2
> To ¼ bowl toddy   4½ "

The broken chair was duly mended at Allen's cost, for some days later there is entered upon the book: "Samuel Allen, Cr. By paying Natt. Heath for mending my arm chair, 3s." But all of his customers do not make such purchases; even goodman Bicknell mixes his rum and religion, and stands charged:

> " To 2 Qts W. Rum   0   1   9
> To 1 Bowl Toddy   0   0 10
> To 1 Psalm book   0   4   0 "

Another literary inclined townsman buys *"the history of King Philip's War"* at three shillings; another *"the Manuel Exercise;"* another buys a spelling book, while nearly all, at the coming in of the new year, buy either *Bickerstaff's* or *West's Almanacks.*

Gingerbread seems to have been a staple article at Bowen's store, and he sells it by the barrel, "rol," and cake. When sold by the barrel it is usually for ship's stores, but most of his trade in this article was by the cake and usually accompanied some liquor, as

" Josiah Viall   Dr

To 1 pt N Rum	o	o	4
To 5 Rols ginger bread	o	o	1½ "

or

" John Harding   Dr

To ½ gil Rum	o	o	2
To 1 Gil Rum	o	o	4
To 2 Qts N Rum	o	1	2½
To 2 Cakes ginger bread @ 4d	o	o	8 "

Here is a charge which shows the care with which he noted down the minute details of his dealings.

" Benjamin Jackson of Rehoboth   Dr

To cash not paid for things you took on Asa Bicknells acct more than y^r order which you Promised to pay if sd Bicknell wood not allow it	o	o	9¾ "

There was to be no dispute when neighbor Bicknell exhibited some surprise at the amount which his friend Jackson had drawn on his order, and here is another:

" Matthew Allen   Dr

To 1 mug flip Dld Timothy Allen the 21st Last Jany which you promised to pay if he did not in one week	o	o	9 "

And Timothy Allen did not respond in the allotted time and this charge is made "Feby. 26, 1772."

The housewife frequently drops into the store for sundry purchases, and the charges made on such occasions seem strange enough in these days when the articles had are considered.

" Hannah Adams   Dr

To 8 Rows of Pins	o	o	2¾ "

and on another occasion,

" 5½ yds Dowlas @ 1s 2d	8	8½ "

and

" Rebecca Brown   Dr

To 1½ yds Quality @ 2d	o	o	3 "

It is doubtful if Squire Bowen meant exactly what he wrote when he made this entry:

"Israel Barney of Swansy   Dr

To my scow one day taken from
yr own mouth   o   2   6 "

for this "scow" was used for such purposes as "loading Cromell Childs schooner," "freighting 1 Bbl of ginger bread & 1 of Biskit," and "loading marsh hay." The charges for entertainment at his taven are here recorded. Breakfast was 9d, while dinner at the tavern was is, 2½d, with a bowl of grog it was is, 6½d. Most of his guests had their dinner at this latter named price.

John Tripp and his wife put up at the inn on the 11th of May, 1776, and the "score" which undoubtedly he settled "without higgling," illustrates the customs of the times as well as conveys a perfect idea of the expense of putting up at one of the old Colonial Inns for a day or so:

"To 1 Dinner 9d To Bread and cheese 6d   1   3
To 2 mugs cyder 1½d To 1 gill W. Rum 4   5½
To breakfast & dinner is 3d To one
    bowl Toddy 9d   2
To lodging you and wife   6
To 1½ bowl toddy is 1½ To ½ mug cyder 1½d   1   3
To lodg self & wife 6d To 1 gil Brandy 5½d   11½
To breakfast 9½d mug cider 1½   11
To ½ bowl toddy 4½d Dinner 8d   1   0½
To 15 lbs Tobacco @ 6d   7   6
To ¼ bowl Toddy 4½d To ½ mug cyder 1½   6
To supper   6"

In the family record which goodman Bowen caused to be spread upon the town books, it is stated that his "fifth child was buried near his mother, who died October 30, 1778." On this old day book there is written, under this date:

"William Kelley   Cr

By 1 coffin   12s "

Every other word on the page on which this is written is in the familiar handwriting of Henry Bowen. This was written by another hand. It was a sad day to the taverner, for death had entered the inn an unwelcome guest, and departing, had taken away its mistress. He remained a widower for seven months, and then, as the record says, "married his second wife, Elizabeth Harding, May 2, 1779," and Elizabeth took the place made vacant, "to welcome the coming and speed the parting guest."

For nearly fifteen years Bowen conducted the tavern and store at Barrington, but in the latter part of the year 1783 he sold out a good part of his belongings at "Vandoo," gave up the inn and all the offices to which he had held so tenaciously, and removed to Providence, where he embarked in business on a more elaborate scale.

There was yet another cheerful, happy day for tavern keepers that has not yet been referred to, and this was Ordination Day, when the minister was settled over the parish. The tavern then was the centre of activity, a special brew of beer was prepared for such occasions called "Ordination beer," while the "Ordination ball" was the social event of the season.

The records of the ancient churches disclose; a habit and custom which prevailed on such occasions, when roast meats, gingerbread, cider, punch and grog constituted the main item of expense attending these services. The historians of these churches have with great unanimity avoided any reference to them in their recital of events connected with the life of the church. Mrs. Earle in her *Sabbath in Puritan New England*, has resurrected from old diaries and other contemporary writings many quaint illustrations of the customs on such occasions. She gives the bill of one tavern keeper in Hartford for entertainment furnished at such a time:

	£	s	d
" To Keeping Ministers	0	2	4
2 Mugs tody	0	5	10
5 Segars	0	3	0
1 Pint Wine	0	0	9
3 lodgings	0	9	0
3 bitters	0	0	9
3 breakfasts	0	3	6
15 boles punch	1	10	0
24 dinners	1	16	0
11 bottles wine	0	3	6
5 mugs flip	0	5	10
5 boles punch	0	6	0
3 boles tody	0	3	6 "

And "This all Paid for except the Ministers Rum," as the bill is quaintly indorsed.

With so many attractive days in the tavern calendar, with so much sociability, jollity and conviviality about his house, no wonder that the tavern keeper was generally good natured and his place a favorite resort, and he could truthfully call attention to his place as furnishing "Food for the Hungry, Drink for the Thirsty, and a Home for the Weary Traveller."

Chapter Six - Tavern Tales and Travellers

STORIES illustrative of all phases of life are associated with the tavern. Tragedies and comedies have here been enacted. Romance, with all its various shades of love, joy and sorrow, cluster around it. It is not necessary to depend upon imaginary or fanciful details to tell the tales of the wayside inn, for there is enough in the real life of the people to give these stories interest, and yet not overstep the bounds of truth.

On September 26, 1671, Goodman Ayers of Brookfield, or, as it was called in those days, Quawbaug, was granted a license "to keep an ordinary, and sell wine and liquor." Regularly each year his license was renewed, until the year 1675-6, so eventful to many New England towns.

Ayers' tavern was located in the centre of the little settlement, and was the most substantial of any of its neighbors. Unusual attention had been paid to its construction, for it served the double purpose of tavern and garrison house, for Quawbaug was a frontier town and in the midst of the Indian country. Directly across the road was the meeting house, where Parson Younglove preached to the people of Brookfield on all church occasions, and at other times worked in the fields and hunted in the woods, to eke out a living in this wilderness. The people were slow in contributing their mite to the pittance which had been agreed upon for his salary, and even goodman Ayers, the most thrifty of the townsmen, refused to pay "for the maintenance of Mr. Younglove, on account that he keeps the ordinary, and has for time past, and should be free from it;" so it is recorded in the annals of the old town.

Brookfield, at this early day, was not a populous or prosperous settlement. The train band could not boast of a commissioned officer, and was commanded, when it had occasion to be commanded at all, by goodman Ayers himself, by virtue of his appointment to the office of Sergeant. Thus affairs went on in the town, uneventful and uninterrupted by outside influence, until the outbreak of that bloody Indian trouble, which has since been handed down in history as King Philip's war. Startling stories of Indian hostilities had reached the ears of the good people of Brookfield from time to time, but they had not taken the news seriously at heart, and had little fear that any trouble would befall them.

The depredations of the Indians and their continuous hostile movements had been brought to the attention of the Colony authorities, and in order to treat with the savages for a peaceful solution of the difficulties, Captain Edward Hutchinson of Boston was commissioned by the General Court to proceed to the neighborhood of Brookfield "to treat with several sachems in those parts in order to the public peace." He therefore set out from Cambridge on the 28th of July, 1675, having an escort of twenty men under the command of Captain Thomas Wheeler, who had also "been ordered by said council to accompany him with part of my troops for security from any danger that might be from the Indians, and to assist him in the transaction of matters committed to him."

This body of men arrived at Brookfield after a march of three days, on the first day of August, when they halted and immediately made an attempt to treat with the savages. When the news of the arrival of the force reached Brookfield some of the townsmen joined with them, prominent among whom was Sergeant Ayers, the chief military man of the town and landlord of the tavern.

Messengers were dispatched to the main body of the Indians, variously estimated from two to five hundred, and it was arranged that the two parties should meet for a discussion of the subject in hand "upon a plain three miles from Brookfield," at 8 o'clock the next morning. Promptly at the time appointed the commissioner and his followers were on hand, but the Indians did not appear. Through the influence of the Brookfield men, who assured the party that the Indians had no evil intentions, it was decided to go to them since they had failed to meet their appointment. The troops therefore set out for the main camp of the savages, which was located in the midst of a thick swamp. Doubtless this was just what the wily heathen had intended for them to do, for no sooner had they reached the swamp, — the way to it being "so very bad that they could only march single file," — when the Indians made a savage attack upon them from ambush. In this attack Sergeant John Ayers was killed. The thoroughly frightened and demoralized troops scattered and fled to the town. The news of the Indians' treachery and the loss of so many men, — for eight men had been killed and five wounded, — spread quickly throughout the settlement. Many of the families hurriedly left their homes, and, with the soldiers, took up quarters in Ayers' tavern, where they proceeded to fortify themselves as best they could. Encouraged by their success in this dastardly attack in the swamp, the Indians started in pursuit of the fleeing townsmen and soldiers, and arrived at the settlement almost as soon as they did.

Through the afternoon the savages occupied their time with stray shots at the besieged townsmen and in pillaging the deserted houses and desecrating the meeting house. "That night," says Captain Wheeler, in his narrative, "they did war against us like so many wild bulls, sending in their shot amongst us till towards the moon rising which was about three of the clock; at which time they attempted to fire our house by hay and other combustible matter which they brought to one corner of the house and set it on fire." Under the protection of the guns, a party ventured outside and succeeded in quenching the flames before they had communicated with the house, but two of the party were wounded by the enemy's shots, which "pierced the walls and flew among the inmates." Fearing that their ammunition and provisions would be exhausted before help could reach them, for there were eighty-two persons, men, women and children shut up in this house. Captain Wheeler decided that, with all the danger attending it, a messenger must be dispatched to Boston for assistance. He therefore selected Ephraim Curtis, a young man thirty-three years of age, who had accompanied the expedition as a guide and interpreter. Twice did this brave fellow attempt to steal away from the besieged tavern, but each time the alert savages discovered him and he was forced to return. On the third attempt he succeeded in stealing away. Boston was between sixty and seventy miles distant, but, says Captain Wheeler, "through God's mercy, he got safely to Marlborough, though very much spent and ready to faint by reason of want of sleep before he went from us, and his sore travel night and day in that hot season till he got thither from whence he went to Boston." Meanwhile the Indians kept up their attack, and the brave defenders of the tavern, without rest and hardly without time for food, struggled against their ferocious enemy trusting that they might hold out until succor arrived. During the daylight the Indians were less demonstrative, which afforded the cooped-up men in the tavern some slight rest, but as darkness came on the savages renewed their attack with the greatest boldness and intensity. "They also used several strategems to fire us," says Wheeler, "namely by wild fire on cotton and linen rags with brimstone in them which rags they tyed to the piles of their arrows sharp for the purpose and shot them to the roof of our house after they had set them on fire which would have much endangered the burning thereof, had we not used means by cutting holes through the roof and otherwise to beat the said arrows down and God being pleased to prosper our endeavors therein. They carried more combustible matter, as flax and hay, to the sides of the house, and set it on fire, and then flocked apace towards the door of the house, either to prevent our going forth to quench the fire, as we had done before, or to kill our men in their attempt to go forth or else to break into the house by the door, whereupon we were forced to break down the wall of the house against the fire to put it out." All through that long and weary night all of the energies of the men were exerted to their highest pitch to resist the various modes of attack by which the cunning savages sought to take their lives. Shortly after daybreak on Wednesday, the fourth of August, the Indians resorted to a new plan and fortified themselves at the meeting house, and at the barn adjoining the tavern. Here they constructed a rude breastwork or barricade of boards, rails and hay. At night they dragged one of the farm carts from the barn, and filling it with "flax hay and candlewood," set it on fire and pushed it against the tavern, using much ingenuity in their method of constructing this appliance to save themselves from harm. Happily for the worn out people in the house it rained that night and so dampened the woodwork and combustibles that the flames did not take effect. Had it not been for this, there is little doubt but what the brave body of defenders of the tavern would have been forced to surrender, and throw themselves into the hands of the merciless savages. The men and women, too, were nearly exhausted, six of their number were incapacitated and suffering from wounds, while the smoke of burning wood, brimstone and powder filled the house, almost stifling them. Besides this, since they had been locked up in this house, their number had been increased by four, two women having given birth to twins. Surely they were in a desperate position, but it is said "'tis always darkest before daybreak," and so it proved, for along in the night of the third day of the siege. Major Willard and Captain Parker, of Groton, with a body of forty-six men and five friendly Indians, arrived upon the scene and put an end to further hostilities. They had heard the news of the attack on Brookfield, and hastily getting together a force, had set out to aid their brethren.

Three days later the help which Ephraim Curtis had sought also arrived, and thus secured the men of Brookfield from danger. During the attack the town was practically wiped out of existence, nothing remaining of this once happy and peaceful settlement except this ruinous old tavern and another building "that was not then finished," and with this bitter experience Ayers' tavern for the entertainment of travellers, and goodman Ayers, who declined to pay the minister's rate, passed into history.

David Fairbanks of Medfield was a tavern keeper and also kept the country store; he was the most energetic business man in the place and broadened his fields of usefulness by embarking in an industry which was destined to grow into great proportions. He was the pioneer in the straw goods business and acquired a considerable property by this means. Conceiving the idea that the spare time of the young women of the town might be put to greater good than gossiping brought them, he purchased large quantities of straw braid, distributed it around among the young girls and women, and for a reasonable compensation employed them to sew it into bonnets and hats. He found a ready market for his goods in New York, sending them overland by ox teams to Providence and thence by packet to New York. From this small beginning the straw goods industry grew to be a large and profitable business in this town.

Not many years ago there was a little coterie of persons in Medfield who produced no end of fun and amusement for the towns people by a curious custom which they inaugurated, of applying to different persons in the village high sounding titles and names of important and celebrated personages. Mr. Onion, the dignified postmaster, was dubbed the "Emperor." James Clark, the good-natured, portly tavern keeper, was styled the "Alderman," while others bent under such weighty titles as "Pope," "Count," "Marshal Ney," "Marshal Marmont," and others equally as grand.

The derivation of these titles too was as curious as the custom itself, for one member of this dignified body having ventured out in a "large tub to gather floating cranberries," unfortunately capsized the frail craft and was thrown bodily into the water, and upon emerging from this impromptu bath was immediately given the rank of "Admiral."

The leader in this club of humorists seems to have been Mr. Onion, the postmaster and store keeper, and he issued his mandates to the others in the most pompous manner. On necessary occasions he furnished bulletins of current news and gossip all in the same style. One day there came to the town two itinerant pedlars of various wares, and by the cheapness of their goods and their persistency in advocating they succeeded in disposing of a good stock to the villagers. Such an invasion was frowned upon by the village store keepers, and especially by Mr. Onion, the "Emperor," but in addition to this usurpation of the rights and privileges of the village merchants, and to their surprise these two unpopular foreign traders found shelter, comfort and cheer at the tavern of James Clark, the popular "Alderman" of the circle. Such a disregard for the feelings of the other villagers could not be tolerated and it was considered the proper time for a manifesto to be issued. This the "Emperor" proceeded forthwith to do, in the following grandiloquent manner:

"Headquarters, September 14.

Sir: — It has fallen to our allottment to behold our hitherto peaceful community in a state of complete anarchy and contention, occasioned by the influx of pedlars. The invading forces from Foxboro and other places encamped with Alderman Clark, who immediately engaged in their service with his usual ardor.

The affairs of the day were conducted with much order and regularity until about 5 o'clock P. M. Then the invading forces, finding they were losing ground, withdrew for the night, giving notice of their intention to resume business in the morning at private sale. Consequently, the Hotel was transformed into a peddling shop. What a degrading scene to witness in our once splendid Tuileries!

Yesterday ended; but this morning I was up early, walking the street, watching the splendor of the sun of Austerlitz, when my attention was attracted to the palace above named to view the appearance of Alderman Clark, one of the *belligerents* pointing to a splendid sign board on his chimney top, and raving in a furious manner to Johnson and others, which drew me to the front. I looked up, and read, in large, well-painted letters:

Pedler's Home, Kept by J. Clark,

on which the worthy Alderman was declaiming.

This war is now not to be avoided. A declaration and manifesto are issued; and eternal wrath threatened on all concerned in erecting the banner, particularly J. H. B. and C. F. Your humble servant is in for his usual share of condemnation and suspicion of projection. We are all now under arms, and are negotiating for the former usual libation to be handed over on raising a sign. All such reasonable demands are, however, treated with contempt. I regret much that you are absent; trust you will hasten home speedily, your services are wanted. Have sent express for W. Janes, as we must carry the garrison by *storm* to correspond with its defence.

I am in haste, the stage is at the door.

Yours in haste,
EMPEROR.

To Marshal Le Brun."

Such proceedings as these produced no end of fun for those within the little circle, and even for those without, for these men were as well, if not better known, by these titles than by their own names, and it is a fact that the printed report of the town's finances for the year 1849 contains this item of expense paid by the town: "Emperor, for postage, $1.53." The postmaster was better known by that name than by his real one, Mr. Onion.

There are no more pathetic stories connected with Colonial life in New England than those that tell of the sufferings experienced and the cruelties inflicted for conscience sake.

Associated with an old tavern which was formerly located at Ipswich is the name of Lydia Wardwell. It was for a brief time only she breathed the air that surrounded it but that short time was filled with torture to her body inflicted by the hard-hearted Puritan townsmen, accustomed to persecute and punish that sect to which she belonged, called Quakers.

Lydia Wardwell was the wife of Eliakim Wardwell of Hampton, and is described as being a "young and tender chaste woman." About the year 1663 she had separated from the church at Newbury where she had formerly worshipped, and had united with the Quakers. In those days withdrawing from the Puritan church was a most serious and horrible offence, and she was commanded to return and explain her conduct in so doing. At last she did so, and imbued with that Quaker purity and fearlessness, "and as a sign to them she went in (though it was exceeding hard to her modest and shamefaced disposition) naked amongst them." The anger of the Puritan church people was aroused to its highest pitch at this act, and she was roughly laid hands on and forcibly ejected from the Newbury meeting house. She then returned to her home at Hampton. Meanwhile the elders of the church, with all the bitterness and harshness that characterized their acts in the persecution of her sect, had considered her conduct, and at the next term of the court at Ipswich she was presented for her misconduct, and under the date of May 5, 1663, there may be found on the records of this court, yet preserved at Salem, this entry: "Lydia Wardwell on her presentment for coming naked into Newbury meeting house. The sentence of the court is, that she shall be severely whipt and pay the costs and fees to the Marshal of Hampton for Bringing her. Costs ten shillings, fees two shillings and sixpence," and the order of the court was obeyed, for she was presently taken in charge by the officers and conducted to the most public spot in the town, in front of the tavern. Here she was "tyed to the fence post of the tavern," and then sorely lashed "with twenty or thirty stripes," while a crowd of people gazed upon this cruel treatment. "And this," said George Bishop in his *New England Judged by the Spirit of the Lord*, "is the discipline of the church in Newbury in New England, and this is their religion, and their usage of the handmaid of the Lord, who in a great cross to her natural temper came thus among them, a sign indeed significatory enough to them, and suitable to their state, who under the visor of religion were thus blinded into cruel persecution." Another such occurrence is associated with the "Anchor Tavern" at Swampscott, where three Rhode Island men were incarcerated on the occasion of their visit to a sick and aged townsman, one William Witter, in July, 1651. These men were Dr. John Clark, John Crandall, and Obadiah Holmes, all prominent men in the Rhode Island colony, and all of the Baptist persuasion.

They arrived at the Swampscott settlement on or about the twentieth of July, the day being Sunday, and went at once to the home of their friend Witter. Here they held religious services, and Dr. Clarke preached to the company assembled, and afterwards, it is said, administered the sacrament. This irregularity in the midst of the Puritan bay colony was soon brought to the attention of the authorities, and a warrant was sworn out by Magistrate Robert Bridges, of Salem, directing the constables to apprehend them as disturbers of the peace. Two constables were directed thereby "to go to the house of William Witter and so to search from house to house for certain erroneous persons, being strangers and them to apprehend and in safe custody to keep and tomorrow morning at eight o'clock" bring them before the magistrate for examination. With great alacrity the law officers proceeded upon their errand and repaired to Mr. Witter's house. Their arrival is described by Dr. Clarke, who says, "while I was yet speaking, there comes into the house where we were, two constables who with their clamorous tongues makes an interruption, and more uncivilly disturbed us than the pursuivants of the old English Bishops were wont to do." The services were peremptorily brought to a close, and the three visitors were informed that they were under arrest. In the afternoon the three Rhode Islanders were taken to Mr. Whitney's meeting house, where they arrived while the congregation was standing at prayers. The party entered the house in an orderly manner, and were assigned to seats, when they sat down, put on their hats, and "fell to reading," in this way showing their disapproval of the proceedings. At the conclusion of the service Dr. Clarke arose and asked permission to make some remarks, which was refused, and he was commanded to remove his hat. Upon refusing so to do, Magistrate Bridges, who was in the meeting house, ordered the constable to "uncover their heads," who performed this duty without much ceremony.

Under the escort of the constables these three summer visitors were conducted to the "Anchor Tavern," then kept by the impecunious Joseph Armitage, where they were locked up and strongly guarded. Next morning they were brought before Magistrate Bridges, who sent them to jail at Boston. On the last day of the month their trial took place, and the Court of Assistants imposed upon each a fine, Mr. Holmes, thirty pounds, Mr. Clarke twenty, and Mr. Crandall five. Mr. Holmes was a minister, and although the less active in the proceedings which brought them into trouble, had aroused the wrath of the Puritan authorities some time before, by committing some disorders on the Lord's day, viewed from their intolerant standpoint.

Clarke and Crandall were soon out of their troubles, for their fines were paid. Not so with Holmes, he was made of sterner stuff, and for conscience sake he refused to pay his fine or to permit it to be paid by others. For some weeks he remained in jail, refusing to discharge the fine or receive aid from his friends, when in the early part of September, he was brought forth from the prison and publicly whipped. When he arrived at the whipping post and the preparations had been made for punishment, he requested liberty to speak to the people, but the presiding officer, one Flint, whose name seems to have been particularly appropriate to his position, refused his request and instead ordered him to be stripped. Then the executioner stepped forth, his sleeves rolled up, "spat three times in his own hands, that he might not fail to honor justice," took firm hold of the three corded lash and proceeded with the work assigned to him. Governor Joseph Jenckes, of Rhode Island, has left an account of the details attending this scene, and in it says: "Mr. Holmes was whipped 30 stripes and in such an unmerciful manner, that for many days if not some weeks he could not take rest but as he lay upon his knees and elbows, not being able to suffer any part of the body to touch the bed."

"As the man began to lay on the stripes, Holmes said: 'though my flesh should fail, yet my God will not fail.' He then prayed 'Lord lay not this sin to their charge.'"

When he was released, two spectators, John Spur and John Hasel, went up and took hold of his hand to sympathize with him; they had come way from Rhode Island to be with their friend in his misfortune. For this exhibition of sympathy they were each fined forty shillings.

It is also stated that some of his friends, just before the executioner proceeded with the lash, brought to him some wine, which they requested him to drink, but he declined to take it, "lest the spectators should attribute his fortitude to drink."

It is difficult to fully comprehend from this brief recital of the trials and hardships of these men what this trouble was about. The only irregularity which the visitors appear to have committed was in keeping their hats on in meeting, which, at the worst, was hardly serious enough to warrant such fines and punishments. The reason for it, however, is not far to seek, for it lay in the narrow-minded, intolerant rule which governed the affairs in the Colony of Massachusetts Bay. And this is but, one of hundreds of such cases.

Roger Mowry's tavern, at Providence, the first hostelry to be established in the settlement, is still standing, the oldest house now in that city, and is distinguished, among other things, as being the only one at the north end of the town that escaped destruction when Providence was burned, in King Philip's war. Landlord Mowry came from Salem, where he had the distinction of holding the position of "neat herd" to that town. The duties of this office gave into his charge the care of all the town cattle. The custom of the time being to drive the common herd afield during the day, and returning them at night, during the season when the grass was suitable for fodder, his term of office commencing the "fifth of the second month," and to continue eight months; "another sufficient man" was associated with him. A time was fixed when each townsman should have their cattle ready to be driven with the common herd, and those who, from various circumstances, neglected to have theirs ready at the appointed time and place, were obliged to bring them themselves after the herd. For this duty the price was regulated at seven shillings a head for "all except bulls," which compensation was "to be paid in four equal payments, and always one quarter beforehand."

It was in May, 1655, that goodman Mowry was granted a license to keep a house of entertainment, and was directed to "sett out a convenient signe at ye most perspicuous place of ye saide house thereby to give notice to strangers that it is a house of entertainment."

It is unfortunate that no record exists as to the name or device which must have appeared upon this sign so conspicuously displayed.

In the early days of the town's life this house was a prominent point. It served many purposes too as the tavern generally did, here the people of the settlement assembled and discussed the news, here the town council held its sessions and voted payment to the landlord for his entertainment in these words, "that ye Treasurer pay to Roger Moorie is 6d out of the Treasurie for this days firing and house room."

Here too Roger Williams held service for the worship of God, for in the Providence settlement for many years there was no meeting house, and religious services were conducted in private houses or at the tavern.

This old house is full of historic interest and many quaint stories of early life in the town centre around it. But it is of a tragedy that occurred near it that is to be here related. Among the members of the household of Roger Williams, that fearless expounder of the doctrine of soul liberty, was a young Dutch lad named John Clawson. Williams in his wanderings had come across this young fellow in a half-naked and starving condition, and seeing his friendless and pitiable state had taken him to his home, where he served his benefactor as a household servant.

He grew to man's estate, acquired a tract of land whereon he built a house, and served the townsmen at his trade of carpenter.

One winter morning in 1660, Clawson was found in a dying condition near a clump of barberry bushes, at the parting of the paths, not far from Roger Mowry's tavern, and he was tenderly carried to the house of Williams, where after some hours of intense suffering, for his head was cut as with a broad axe, he died, surrounded by many of his friends and neighbors, including Williams and his wife and Elizabeth Hernden, "Goode Wickenden," and Mistress Throckmorton. So badly was he injured that it was with difficulty he could speak, but it is said that he imprecated curses upon one of his townsmen named John Hernton, whom he accused of being responsible for this attack, and hoped that all of his children and his children's children would "be marked with split chins and haunted by barberry bushes."

Meanwhile a search was instituted to find the murderer, and as it was the first crime to be committed in the settlement, of so serious a nature, the greatest excitement prevailed throughout the town. It was not long before suspicion was directed to one Waumanitt, an Indian, and he was therefore apprehended and taken to the tavern of Roger Mowry, where he was locked up and securely guarded. Gradually, little by little, the story of the murder came to light; all that is definitely known of it to-day is what tradition has handed down, and is to this effect.

Clawson, while leisurely walking along the upper end of the Town Street, not far from where the tavern was located, passed by a "clump of barberry bushes." As he did so, Waumanitt, who had been in hiding awaiting his approach, sprang upon him, and with an axe, clove his head.

Tradition also tells the story that the murder was instigated by one John Hernden, one of the townsmen, who had employed the Indian to commit the deed, but for what reason tradition is silent.

Clawson had some little estate, and the town a depleted treasury. In order, therefore, that the expenses attending this affair might be provided for, the town treasurer was directed to take into his hands the property belonging to the dead Dutchman and pay the charges from it, for Clawson is said to have had no kindred. The account of the disbursements from this fund is yet preserved, and it tells many little details of this tragedy that have heretofore been unknown.

In the quiet and peaceful settlement of Providence there had been no provisions made for shackles to bind a murderer. So the services of Henry Fowler, the town blacksmith, were brought into play to make them, and his bill 'for irons" was six shillings and three pence. A guard of nine men, including "the man at Moories," was necessary to watch the prisoner, at three shillings each a night, and for two days and a half this watch was maintained. Stephen Northup, the town constable or town crier, was employed "warning the town about the prisoner," and was paid three shillings for it. Landlord Mowry, "for houseroom for the prisoner," put in a bill of four shillings. Upon the death of Clawson the "Crowner's Quest" was summoned, and the cause of it duly determined.

Then the town meeting was convened to determine what should be done with the Indian, for he was not a welcome guest at the inn. There was no prison or place suitable for prisoners in Providence, for the colony prison was at Newport, and so the meeting voted "that the prisoner Waumanitt shall be sent down unto Newport to the Collony prison There to be kept until his tyme of Triall."

At the preliminary hearing Roger Williams and Valentine Whitman, who were skilled in the Indian language, assisted the authorities in getting at the facts of the case, and the former for "Interpreting once," and the latter for "Interpreting about the prisoner twise," were paid twelve shillings.

A boat was got in readiness to transport the prisoner to the town of Newport, and there was provided "1 pint of liquors for the young men that lancht the Boat," at two shillings six pence. Two of the townsmen, Thomas Walling and Ed. Inman were selected to escort the prisoner, and with "1 pint of liquors to carry with them in the Boat" and "for powder and shott to carry along wth ye prisoner," they set out for Newport thirty miles away. Whether they ever reached Newport or not or what afterwards became of the murderer is not known, for on these points the records are silent.

Among the first to reach the side of the young Dutchman, when he was taken to Williams' house, were Benjamin Hernden and his wife, the father and mother of the alleged instigator of the crime, and they tenderly nursed him and administered "sack and sugar whilst he lay wounded." The general provisions for his funeral were consistent with his position and estate. The special provisions were "5 pints liquors," "Bread and Cheese," these with a "winding sheete" cost £1 2s 6d. For making the coffin and furnishing nails and "2 Trap lines" with which to lower the body into the grave, there was paid five shillings and six pence, and with the simple rites attending his burial, passed from the scenes of the Providence settlement this poor murdered Dutch carpenter. Notwithstanding the suspicion that was directed against Hernden he seems to have continued to dwell in the settlement, and not until the early part of the next century was he gathered to his fathers. The land adjoining the spot where this murder is said to have been committed was some years later laid out for a burying ground, and there are those now living who can remember a dense growth of barberry bushes there by the roadside.

It was, until recent years, a lonely, dark and grewsome spot, and it is related that travellers along the road always whipped up their horses or walked at a more rapid gait, when they reached this place and called to mind the dark deed there committed and the curse of Clawson.

In the early part of the present century the country taverns were the common resort of many of the old soldiers who had served in the American Revolution. Here they would assemble on all occasions and recount their experiences at Bunker Hill, Long Island, Springfield, Monmouth, Brandy wine, and other momentous battles in which they had borne an honorable part. They were always surrounded with a crowd of young men, and even old ones, who stood or sat with attentive ears, listening to their stories of victory, defeat and disaster. Some of the old heroes had formed a habit of deep drinking, and so long as the onlookers and listeners would keep up a supply of liquor to lubricate their vocal organs these stories would fall from their lips just as long as there were ears to listen.

There was an old tavern in New Hampshire which was a favorite resort for such parties, and through the long winter evenings and hot summer days a little coterie of these story tellers could always be found. One of the characters in the village was a young fellow, not over bright, who was the butt of many a joke, and was always found lounging about the tavern. He was known in the village and even for miles around as John Jack, a contraction of his real one, which was Jonathan Jackson Tuttle. Besides imbibing the various beverages which the tavern bar supplied, he had also imbibed all these stories which he had heard, and so familiar had he become with the various episodes of the war that he could tell these oft-repeated tales as well as many of the veterans. But this was not the worst of it, for so familiar had these details of the Revolutionary struggle become to him that he at last repeated them as his own experiences. The villagers encouraged him in this, until finally he was as firm in his belief that he, too, had fought in the Revolution, as any of the old heroes themselves.

One day there came to the village a gentleman from another town on a visit to one of the townsmen, and in the course of showing him about the place they entered the tavern one hot summer afternoon and found the little knot of heroes discussing the various phases of the war, prominent among whom was John Jack, talking as loud and as earnestly as any of them. Somewhat surprised to hear the young man talking so knowingly of events which had transpired long before he was born, the visitor turned to his companion and asked him what kind of a character this young fellow was. Without replying to his question, he looked up into his face, gave a significant wink and said, "John, do you remember the battle of the Brandywine:

"Wall I dew," drawled the youth, "I remember that day bettern' all the others for I fought pretty much all by myself that day along with Gineral Washington. Yer see our comp'ny was in the lead an when the Britishers begin to fire on us lots o' our fellows just cut an run, they did. Seeing as I was pretty much alone I jest crawled along by an old stone wall by an apple orchard and scrouched down in a corner and there I sot.

"There was lots of fightin' goin' on all around but I gest sot right there and peppered away at the red coats pretty much all the morning and say I must a killed mor'n twenty on em for ev'ry time I fired I seen a red coat drop. Wall, along in the afternoon, bout three o'clock, who should come ridin' down right near where I sot, but Gineral Washington settin on a big white horse, and when he seen me, he pulled up his horse and with a wave of his hand says, 'John what you doin down here all alone by yourself.?' I says 'Gineral; fightin, fightin for my country I've been here pretty much all day and I've killed mor'n twenty on em.'

"'John' he says and he looked down at me so pleasant like, John' he says 'you've served your country well to day. You'd better go to your tent and rest.'

"'No Gineral,' says I, 'I can't do that, my country needs me right here every minute' John,' he says, and he looked down agin so pleasant like, 'John, don't call me Gineral, call me George.'"

A hearty laugh followed the recital of this story, and after supplying the would be revolutionary hero with a draught at the bar, the party withdrew.

It is also related that an ancient townsman, who was classed among the habitues of the tavern, and who was obliged to limp about with a cane, was always alluded to as a survivor of the revolution, for the injuries which produced his lameness were received on an over shot water wheel which he was engaged in repairing.

The romance of the "Fountain" inn is, perhaps, the best known and the most interesting of any of the tales of the taverns. The poet has sung it in charming verse, the novelist has woven it into a delightful story, while the historian has found ample material for a valuable monograph in colonial history.

If ever you go to that even-to-day quaint old seaport town of Marblehead you cannot fail to hear the name of Agnes Surriage; indeed, you are more apt to hear the name of this peculiarly fortunate weak woman, who lived there in her girlhood, than you are to hear the names of many of those old-time worthies, who added lustre to the history of the town, for the story of a weak woman has outlived in many cases the heroic acts on land and sea of the men of Marblehead, and the old well which stood beside the "Fountain" inn has many more visitors than the house where dwelt that staunch old patriotic Elbridge Gerry.

If you go over to the "Neck," among the broad piazzas overlooking the bay, you will find the summer guests in little groups telling the story of Agnes Surriage, and pointing to the ruins of old Fort Sewall, across the harbor. On the counters of the shops in the town you will find Bynner's charming story of her life. The guidebook points out the location of the tavern, and if you stroll down upon the ramparts of the old fort, linked so closely with her memory, you will find cut deeply into one of the wooden benches, the names, "Agnes Surriage" and "Harry Frankland."

Near the foot of Burying Hill, on a lane running from the main street of the town. stood the "Fountain" inn, presided over by goodman Salkins. Up the hill was the little graveyard, and close beside this was the meeting house, while stretching down towards the sheltered harbor was the little settlement of hardy fishermen. The "Fountain" inn was the most popular, if not the only, public house, in the town, and was a favorite resort for the townspeople, — mostly seafaring men, — who here discussed the prospects of the next catch at the "Banks," and drank with each other over their stories of the sea.. The tap room at the "Fountain" was a most inviting spot, as the liquors which were there dispatched were of the finest quality, for it is said many a cargo of Spanish wine was smuggled into the little port, and the smugglers themselves found shelter within the tavern.

Infrequently there would come to the town, dignitaries of the colony brought there on official business, and on such occasions the "Fountain" was even more of an attractive spot than usual.

One day in the fall of 1742 there came to the tavern a traveller, who announced himself as Sir Harry Frankland; he was directly from the town of Boston where he occupied the position of Collector of the Port. His visit, it is said, was in connection with the fort then in process of construction on the point.

While stopping at the inn he chanced to fall into conversation with one of the servants at the house, a young girl of fifteen years, whose striking personality very much impressed him. She was barefooted, down upon her knees engaged in scrubbing the floor, dressed in the coarsest of ill-fitting apparel. As she looked up and turned her face toward him and replied to his questions, the exquisite mouldings of her features and the charming music of her voice filled him with astonishment and admiration.

Such beauty and grace in one so lowly circumstanced he had never witnessed, and so interested did he become in this fair young girl that he prolonged the conversation. At last, noticing the bare feet showing beneath her petticoat, he asked her why she did not wear her shoes. To which the young maid replied that she had none. Pitying her poverty and impressed with her face he took from his pocket a piece of money, telling her to use it to purchase a pair of shoes. During his stay his thoughts reverted frequently to this illiterate and destitute servant girl, until, so curious did he become, that he made inquiries of the tavern keeper and ascertained that her name was Agnes Surriage, the daughter of a reputable fisherman in the town named Edward Surriage. The business which brought him to the fishing town was soon over, and Frankland left for Boston. Some time after this Frankland again had business which called him to Marblehead, but whether it was the building of the fort, or the visions of this beautiful face, would be difficult to decide. He repaired at once, however, to the old inn, where, busily engaged in the drudgery of the house, he saw again the fair creature who was destined to play such an important part in the drama of his life.

She was clad pretty much as he had at first found her, and her feet were without shoes or stockings. Noticing this presently, he asked her if she had not used the money which he had given her for the shoes, and was answered that she had, but that she was keeping them to wear to meeting. To Frankland there was an irresistible attractiveness in the beauty and personality of this young girl, and ere he made his departure from the town, he had arranged with her parents to take her to Boston, there to be educated.

The fact that he obtained her parents' consent for such an undertaking is most remarkable. Frankland at this time was but twenty-six years of age, only older by ten years than the young woman whom he took for his ward, and the great difference in the positions occupied by each would seem to have prompted a refusal to such a request at once. Doubtless amazed, bewildered and confused at so startling a proposition, her parents had not the force to calmly consider the question, and the request was promptly granted.

Frankland escorted the young girl to Boston, where, true to his word, she was soon settled at her studies. He employed private tutors, who instructed her in music, dancing, painting, and the common branches of learning; and such aptness for these did she display, that in a few years her intellectual advancement had kept pace with her increased womanly charms, and "the poor servant girl of the tavern became the one absorbing subject of conversation in the fashionable circles of Boston."

Such a condition of affairs as existed between these two young people did not pass unnoticed by the people of Boston. Frankland was too prominent a personage in the social life of the town to escape the tongue of scandal, and old matrons busied themselves with the stories which came to their ears, and the young women whispered their suspicions to each other. It was not long before "charges of improper intimacy were freely made, and with Puritanic firmness the polite society of the town refused to recognize one whom they believed to be guilty of transgressing the most holy laws of God and man."

Gradually but surely the two were ostracised from all society until life in Boston became so unbearable that Frankland resolved to take his protege to some secluded spot in the country, away from the carping criticism of his associates. Public opinion was too much against him for a comfortable home in Boston. Nearly nine years had now passed since he had taken this woman to his care. In 1751, having selected a farm tract of four hundred and eighty-two acres in the town of Hopkinton, he erected a magnificent mansion. The house formerly stood on the old road from Ashland to Hopkinton, but about the year 1857 it was totally destroyed by fire.

Dr. Nason, who owned the house at the time of its destruction, thus describes it: "It stood at some distance from the main road, and was approached by a noble avenue cut through the chestnut forest, and by a flower garden tastefully arranged in front. The spacious hall, sustained by fluted columns, was hung with tapestry richly ornamented with dark figures, on a ground of deepest green, according to the fashion of the times. The chimney pieces were of Italian marble, and cornices of stucco work and other costly furnishing embellished the parlor, ante-rooms and chambers."

Everything surrounding the establishment was on the same elaborate and substantial plan, the barns and outbuildings were commodious and finely equipped, while fruit trees of every kind and flower beds embellished the grounds.

Notwithstanding the ill-favor in which they had been situated, the house at Hopkinton seems to have been the resort of the "*elite* of Boston," and parties and assemblies enlivened their days at the Hopkinton mansion, and here they lived for three years, surrounded with all that wealth could supply. Slaves waited upon them, of whom Frankland had quite a retinue, rejoicing in such names as Jacinta, Bacchus, Cato, Dinah, and several others. These three years were noteworthy ones to the people of the little town in those days, and even now are not altogether lost to memory by the people of Hopkinton.

Business of an important character took Frankland to England in 1754, and with him went the young woman who had so many years been his companion. Doubtless Frankland thought that the queenly grace and great beauty of Agnes would gain for her admission to the social life of his native land and that she would be received by his people with open arms. The irregularities of his life, however, had preceded him, and Agnes was no more welcomed in England than she had been in Boston, and no amount of solicitation and excuses could gain for her admission to that select social world in which his people moved. Wearied at last with the situation, yet still devoted to his mistress, he resolved to make a tour of Europe. By a strange fatality which seems to have followed the couple through their lives, they were in Lisbon at the time of the great earthquake in November, 1755.

There is a suspicion that the gay life of the European cities had diminished somewhat the love which Frankland had thus far so devotedly shown for Agnes, for on "All Saints Day," the day of the great calamity to the Portuguese capital, he was riding with a lady on his way to Church. History has failed to chronicle the name of his companion on this fatal day, for with the upheaval which followed the earthquake shock, the falling walls of a building engulfed the carriage, killing his companion and burying carriage, horses and all in the debris. In the midst of the excitement and confusion following the shock, Agnes Surriage rushed from her apartments into the street and mingled with the crowd of terror-stricken people. Her only thought was for the safety of her lover, and while wandering, grief-stricken, aimlessly about the city, she heard a faint voice crying for help coming from beneath the ruins which lined the roadway. She instantly recognized it as the voice of Frankland.

Crying to him to keep up good cheer, she went manfully at work to extricate him, and with the assistance of some of the people about the street, she at last was rewarded by seeing her lover dragged from the mass of ruins not seriously injured. Frankland, during the time while he lay thus imprisoned, had occasion to review the life he had led, and as the full significance of it came upon him, he made a vow before his God that if he was spared "he would thereafter lead a better life."

The injuries which Frankland had received were not severe, but they necessitated his being carried to a neighboring house, where, for some days, he was tenderly nursed by his devoted companion. As soon as he had sufficiently recovered, faithful to this vow he had made, he sent for a priest, and in the city of Lisbon, Agnes Surriage, the former servant girl of the "Fountain" inn at Marblehead, became Lady Agnes Frankland.

When his injuries were healed and his health restored, Sir Harry and Lady Agnes proceeded to England. During the passage, another bit of romance was added to their hitherto romantic life, by a marriage on ship-board, for Frankland, in order to conform to his religious views, was remarried by a clergyman of the Church of England.

Their reception in England was in strange contrast to that which they had received on their former visit.

Her husband's people received her with open arms, and she, who only a short time before had been snubbed and disregarded, now "gained access to the most cultivated and aristocratic circles" of London.

Tired at length with the gaiety and excitement of their London life, and yearning for the scenes so closely identified with their earlier days, the couple sailed again for Boston, where, for some time, they occupied alternately an elegant mansion in that town, and their Hopkinton manor house.

"Though Lady Frankland had thus risen from obscurity to this commanding social position, she did not allow herself to forget her humble origin, or cease to cherish a sister's kind regard for the other members of the family." She contributed much to the comfort of her sisters and brothers, and they were always welcome quests at her home.

Two years after their marriage, and while living in Boston, Frankland received the appointment of consul general at Lisbon, and for six years their residence was in this gay capital, but in 1763, they again returned to their Hopkinton home, but not for that long and happy stay which they had hoped. After a few months at their manor house, Frankland's health became impaired, and again they sailed for England, hoping that the change would benefit him. It was destined to be his last sojourn at the home they had both known so long and well. For five years, with varied stages of hope and despair, Frankland went from place to place, vainly seeking the health he so much desired, when in the year 1768, while sojourning in Bath, to which place he had been recommended, he breathed his last.

Alone, and in the midst of strangers, England had no charms for Lady Frankland, and with a sad heart she again returned to America and established herself at her Hopkinton home. Here, surrounded by her sister and her sister's children, she lived, "respected and beloved by all who knew her," until the outbreak of the war of the Revolution, when alarmed at the aspect of affairs and being more closely wedded to the cause of the crown than that of the colonies, she resolved to return to Boston and seek protection from the British military authority. She therefore asked permission from the Committee of Safety to pass the lines. A pass was readily granted and liberty given her to take with her also, "six trunks, one chest, three beds and bedding for the same, six sheep, two pigs, one small keg of pickled tongues, some hay, three bags of corn and such other goods as she should think proper to carry thither." Armed with her pass she set out for the town; while nearing Boston a company of continentals under the command of Captain Abner Craft, stopped her, and notwithstanding the authority from the Committee of Safety for her passage, she was arrested and held in custody for some time, until at last an order was received for her release. Her journey was continued with a guard of soldiers furnished by order of the Provincial Court, and with this escort she safely reached Boston. Soon after her arrival was fought the battle of Bunker Hill, and this conflict she watched from the windows of her apartments. As soon as the opportunity presented itself, she again set sail for England, and there lived for several years in the family of her late husband. While living there she formed the acquaintance of John Drew, a wealthy banker of Chichester, to whom she was married.

Her eventful life terminated on the twenty-third of April, 1783, at the age of fifty-five years. On her tomb there is this inscription and epitaph:

DAME AGNES FRANKLAND,

RELICT OF

SIR CHARLES HENRY FRANKLAND, BART.,

AND LATE WIFE OF

JOHN DREW,

DIED APRIL 23, 1783,

AGED 55 YEARS.

"Virtue, not rolling Suns, the mind matures,
That life is long which answers life's great end,
The time that bears no fruit, deserves no name.
The man of wisdom is the man of years."

Such is the story of these two lives, and well may it be called the romance of the Fountain inn.

The old tavern at Marblehead in time fell into decay, tumbled down, and was forgotten, save as the townspeople recalled now and then the romantic story which there had its origin, until one day, not many years ago, the old well, which formerly stood in the garden, was accidentally uncovered, and uncovered, too, the history which surrounded it. And to-day the water within it sparkles as brightly and is as sweet to taste as when, long years ago, Agnes Surriage sang by the well sweep, as she filled her bucket with its waters to wash the floors of the Fountain inn.

Chapter Seven - The Tavern in the Revolution

SOME years before the outbreak of the Revolutionary war there might have been found in the tap rooms of the taverns or about their door yards little groups of hardy yeomen intently engaged in discussing the peculiar aspect of affairs in the Colonies.

For generations the people had looked upon the public house as the source of all information, and to it they naturally resorted when such momentous questions agitated their minds. Here their grievances were fully ventilated, and measures of resistance, to British tyranny and oppression, formulated. The tavern was their club, their board of trade, their "exchanges;" and, indeed, to most of the colonists it served as their newspaper.

John Adams noted this widespread feeling of resistance and determination to strike for liberty as he travelled from town to town in the Massachusetts Bay Colony. A conversation which he overheard while drying himself before the fire in the Shrewsbury tavern showed plainly to him, much as he detested the public house, that some sound doctrine was laid down even in the taverns, for he says: "Within the course of the year, before the meeting of Congress in 1774, on a journey to some of our circuit courts in Massachusetts, I stopped one night at a tavern in Shrewsbury, about forty miles from Boston, and as I was cold and wet, I sat down at a good fire in the bar-room to dry my great coat and saddlebags, till a fire could be made in my chamber. There presently came in, one after another, half a dozen, or half a score, substantial yeomen of the neighborhood, who, sitting down to the fire, after lighting their pipes, began a lively conversation on politics. As I believed I was unknown to all of them, I sat in total silence to hear them. One said: 'The people of Boston are distracted.' Another answered: 'No wonder the people of Boston are distracted. Oppression will make wise men mad.' A third said: 'What would you say if a fellow should come to your house and tell you he was come to take a list of your cattle, that Parliament might tax you for them at so much a head? And how should you feel if he was to go and break open your barn to take down your oxen, cows, horses and sheep?' 'What should I say.?'

replied the first, 'I would knock him in the head." 'Well,' said a fourth, 'if Parliament can take away Mr. Hancock's wharf and Mr. Rowe's wharf, they can take away your barn and my house.' After much more reasoning in this style, a fifth, who had as yet been silent, broke out: 'Well, it's high time for us to rebel; we must rebel some time or other, and we had better rebel now than at any time to come. If we put it off for ten or twenty years, and let them go on as they have begun, they will get a strong party among us, and plague us a great deal more than they can now. As yet they have but a small party on their side.'"

Such conversations might have been heard at this period at all the taverns throughout the New England colonies. As early as 1768 the Sons of Liberty were holding their meetings at the public houses, and advocating that freedom and liberty which had prompted their fathers to establish themselves in the wilderness of America.

Captain Joseph Olney, of Providence, with imposing ceremonies dedicated one of the great elms that shaded his tavern as a Liberty Tree. The event was a memorable one to the town, and the formalities attending this dedication were solemn and dignified.

The Olney tavern stood at the top of Constitution Hill, a large old-fashioned, two story, low-studded house, with a large yard in front. "In this yard," says one who remembered well the old place, for it was long since demolished, "stood the largest elm tree that I ever saw. A flight of steps was erected, leading perhaps twenty feet up to where three or four limbs set out. There a convenient seat was fixed for say ten or twelve people to sit in and enjoy themselves in the shade."

On the twenty-fifth day of July, 1768, a large concourse of the townspeople assembled around the spacious yard of the tavern to witness these ceremonies, and lend encouragement by their presence to the principles there enunciated.

The orator on this occasion was Silas Downer, a leading attorney in the town, and standing on this platform in the tree, high above the heads of the people, he delivered a most eloquent discourse, teeming with patriotic and inspiring utterances. After the speaking those assembled reverently laid their hands upon the tree of liberty, while the orator solemnly and impressively pronounced these words: "We do, in the name and behalf of all the true sons of liberty in America, Great Britain, Ireland, Corsica, or wheresoever they may be dispersed throughout the world, dedicate and solemnly devote this tree to be a tree of liberty. May all our councils and deliberations, under its venerable branches, be guided by wisdom, and directed for the support and maintenance of that liberty, which our renowned forefathers sought out and found under trees and in the wilderness. May it long flourish, and may the sons of liberty often repair hither to confirm and strengthen each other; when they look towards this sacred elm, may they be penetrated with a sense of their duty to themselves and to their posterity; and may they, like the house of David, grow stronger and stronger, while their enemies, like the house of Saul, shall grow weaker and weaker. Amen!"

In the long years of uncertainty and doubt which followed, it was the custom for the leading men of the town to assemble here beneath this tree or in the cool shade of its branches, and discuss and lay plans for the success of the cause which they espoused.

Nearly every town throughout the colonies had its Liberty tree or Liberty pole.

A year later, in 1769, John Adams attended one of these gatherings of the Sons of Liberty, and of it thus wrote in his diary, under the date of August 14, 1769: "Dined with three hundred and fifty Sons of Liberty, at Robinsons', the sign of Liberty Tree, in Dorchester. We had two tables laid in the open field, by the barn, with between three and four hundred plates and an awning of sail-cloth overhead, and should have spent a most agreeable day had not the rain made some abatement of our pleasures...This is cultivating the sensations of Freedom. There was a large collection of good company. Otis and Adams are politic in promoting these festivals; for they tinge the minds of the people, they impregnate them with the sentiments of liberty, they render the people fond of their leaders in the cause, and averse and bitter against all opposers. To the honor of the Sons, I did not see one person intoxicated, or near it."

So rapidly had the seeds sown by the Sons brought forth fruit, that in the following year Landlord Woodbridge of the tavern at York, (Me.), boldly emblazoned upon his signboard, which bore the portrait of Mr. Pitt, "**Entertainment for the Sons of Liberty**," and John Adams wrote again in his diary, "Thus the spirit of liberty circulates through every minute artery of the Province." At another time he mentions his stop at Woodburn's tavern in Worcester, and in the course of the evening the conversation turning in the direction of the all absorbing subject of liberty, the landlord sent out for two young ladies who presently appeared and added to the entertainment and enthusiasm of the hour by singing the "New Liberty Song."

As time went on and a peaceful adjustment of the grievances of the colonies became impossible, and war clouds hung dark and low, the taverns were the center of all activity.; Within their walls the Committees of Safety were holding their sessions. The Councils of War were gravely deliberating the great questions laid before them. Recruiting officers had their headquarters in the tap rooms. The town arms were secreted in the tavern chambers.

One of the depositories for the town arms of Smithfield, (R, I.) was at Peleg Arnold's tavern, a house still standing near the Woonsocket line, and within this old inn the Smithfield company of minute men were recruited.

The tavern kept by Increase Newhall at Lynn was one of the alarm stations in this section, where the minute men were ordered to assemble on occasions of emergency.

In 1777 there was a feint made by the British, which has since been known as the "King's Beach alarm." The intelligence was quickly circulated, and the militia men came pouring in from the surrounding country, eager to defend their homes and property from the depredations of the enemy. They left the plough, the shop, and the forge, promptly responded and patiently awaited their commander, who was to lead them to battle. At last they were forced to march away under the command of a subordinate officer.

On the approach of the company the enemy withdrew and the men returned once more to their rendezvous safe and sound, just in time to see their captain emerge from the great brick oven in the kitchen where he had secreted himself when danger threatened. The company after this had little confidence in the valor of their commanding officer.

Weatherby's "Black Horse" tavern was situated on the road between Cambridge and Lexington, at what was then called Menotomy. Here the Province Committees of Safety and Supplies held their meetings. Included among the members of these committees were such men as John Hancock, Samuel Adams, Elbridge Gerry, Azor Orne, Colonel Jeremiah Lee, and General William Heath.

On the eighteenth of April, 1775, these committees had a meeting: of more than usual importance; rumors of an intended attempt co destroy the stores at Concord had reached the ears of the committeemen and measures were considered to secure these invaluable munitions of war against loss.

The session was prolonged till near sunset, when the meeting adjourned. General Heath departed for his home in Roxbury, and while riding along the road toward Lexington was somewhat surprised to see so far from their quarters eight or nine British officers, fully armed, on the road apparently reconnoitring. He made no further investigation of the matter, returned to his home and went to bed, little dreaming of the events of the morrow.

Hancock and Adams went over to Lexington to pass the night. The three Marblehead members of the body, Orne, Lee and Gerry, resolved to remain that night at Weatherby's. Along in the evening, as they sat by the tavern windows, they noticed from time to time small parties of British soldiery passing the house. Their suspicions were excited, and believing that such movements were with hostile intent, Gerry sent a messenger over to Lexington, informing Hancock and Adams of what had been seen. Nothing unusual occurred before bedtime, and these three patriots, thoughtless of any personal danger, retired to their rooms and soon slept. Shortly after midnight they were suddenly awakened by one of the *attaches* of the tavern, who excitedly informed them that a large body of British troops were within sight of the house. Hurriedly jumping from their beds and hastily putting on some of their clothing, they went to the window and looked out. It was a clear, cold, moonlight night, and outlined sharp and distinct they saw the dark line of regulars steadily marching up the road, the polished steel of their arms glittering and flashing where the moonbeams glanced upon them. So intently did they watch this strange proceeding that the troops were before the tavern before they fully realized it, and not until a squad of soldiers entered the tavern yard and approached the house did they think of personal danger. Then it came flashing through their minds that the British had doubtless learned of the meeting the day before and were taking steps to prevent another.

Hastily descending from their chambers half-dressed, they left the tavern by one of the rear doors, and undiscovered by the soldiers, secreted themselves in a field adjoining the house; here for more than an hour they shivered and shook in the chill April morning air, until the soldiers, failing to discover their whereabouts, left the tavern. "Every apartment of the house was searched for the members of the Rebel Congress. Even the beds in which they had lain were examined, but their clothing and other property, including a valuable watch of Mr. Gerry's which was under his pillow was not disturbed."

Upon the withdrawal of the troops the refugees returned to the tavern, chilled through from exposure. It was a fatal night to Colonel Lee, for he "was soon after attacked with a severe fever which resulted in his death."

The battle of Lexington was fought that morning, and for many years was waged that sanguinary conflict which finally resulted in American Independence.

While Landlord James Olney was entertaining the Sons of Liberty under the shade of his Liberty tree at the north end of the town of Providence, there was meeting at another tavern at the south end of the town another body of patriots. They met but once, but the act resulting from that meeting was of such boldness and daring that it sent a tremor of excitement and wonderment throughout the colonies, for it was the first deliberate, premeditated armed attack against the British crown.

Down along the water front of Providence town among the docks where great Indiamen rose and fell with the tide, James Sabin had a tavern, much resorted to by the seafaring men of the town as well as by the substantial merchants and colony officials. Directly opposite his house was Fenner's wharf, from which a regular packet sailed to New York and to Newport, then a most flourishing sea-port.

On the ninth day of June, 1772, there arrived at this wharf, about sunset, a little sloop called the "Hannah," whereof one Benjamin Lindsey was master. After the captain had securely moored his craft to the dock, he communicated some startling information to the little knot of bystanders who had come down to the wharf to witness the arrival of the packet. While they gathered around him, he excitedly told them, that on his trip up the bay, soon after leaving Newport, he was chased by His Britannic Majesty's schooner "Gaspee," that the chase had continued as far as Namquit Point, where by drawing his pursuer into shallow water, the "Gaspee" had been stranded on the point, and there she lay unable to extricate herself, nor would she until high water at midnight. The news of this cunning of the Hannah's captain and the situation of the craft spread like wild-fire about the town. For months the "Gaspee" had been an annoyance to the commerce and peace of the colony. Her commander, William Duddingston, had, without the slightest authority, stopped all vessels, including market boats, seized many of them, and contrary to all law had sent the vessels so seized to Boston for trial. Not only had he annoyed and interfered with the vessels, but members of his crew had oftentimes landed along the bay-side and robbed and insulted the inoffensive bay-side farmers. So persistently had Duddingston and his crew pursued their illegal and offensive course, that the colonial authorities had taken notice of the matter, and letters between the Governor and the commander of the "Gaspee" had frequently passed, but to no purpose.

Letters were sent to Admiral Montague in command of the British fleet, at Boston, complaining of the acts of Duddingston, and even the home government in England had been apprised of the situation of affairs, but without avail. The British admiral would not withdraw the "Gaspee," and its commander would not respect the law. All of this had so excited the indignation of the colonists that their bitterness against the vessel and her commander had been aroused for months to the highest pitch. The time was now ripe for action. A few of the leading merchants and ship owners discussed gravely the news which Captain Lindsey had brought, and it was determined to destroy the vessel before she could be released from the treacherous sands of Namquit.

Along about dusk that June evening, one of the townsmen, beating a drum, passed up and down the main street, informing the excited inhabitants that the "Gaspee" was aground on Namquit Point and would not float till after midnight, and invited those who felt disposed to take part in her destruction to assemble at James Sabin's tavern.

At nine o'clock that evening Sabin's tavern was a busy place. Outside the house, in the street, the drummer beat his drum and little knots of excited men stood whispering together with determined faces. Inside the tavern, in the southeast room, there was a crowd of men, including many professional men, merchants and shipmasters; it was no irresponsible mob, but a body of educated, deep thinking, determined men.

Nearly every man had a gun, powder horn and bullet pouch. Around the fireplace men were melting lead and running it into bullets, others were oiling the locks of their guns, and seeing that their arms were in good order. By ten o'clock the room was filled with people, when with a whispered order from someone in authority the party silently filed out of the tavern, crossed the street to Fenner's wharf, and dropped, one by one, into eight long boats which had been prepared for the expedition.

Silently, and with oars muffled, the fleet of boats passed down the river, nearing at last the location of the stranded vessel, where, looming up before them the occupants of the boats saw

"a huge, black hulk, that was magnified
By its own reflection in the tide."

When within about sixty yards of the "Gaspee," the boats were hailed by the sentinel with "Who comes there?" to which there was no answer. Again he hailed, no reply. The cry of the sentinel had aroused Lieutenant Dudding-ston, the commander, who now appeared upon deck, clad only in his night shirt, and he demanded, "Who comes there?" This was answered by bold Captain Abraham Whipple, who commanded the expedition, with a volley of oaths intermingled with, "I am the Sheriff of the County of Kent," "I have got a warrant to apprehend you," "so surrender."

At the conclusion of this peculiar answer there was the report of a musket, and Duddingston fell to the deck, wounded in the stomach. The boats then closed in, and the party scrambled aboard the doomed vessel. The crew were soon prisoners, and after the wounds of the commander of the "Gaspee" had been treated, the whole ship's crew were rowed ashore and landed at the little village of Pawtuxet, a short distance north of the point. A detachment from the expedition then set the vessel afire, and the annoying, pestiferous craft, which had been for so many months a menace to the colony, was, ere daylight, completely destroyed.

As orderly and deliberately as the expedition had set out it returned to the town, and the members of it silently repaired to their several homes. All of the party were enjoined to the greatest secrecy, and notwithstanding the rig-orous investigation which subsequently followed by a Royal Commission appointed by the King, and the offer of large rewards, not a single person comprising this daring party was ever apprehended. Indeed, not till years after, were the names of the conspirators known, and only those of a very few are known to this day.

In the early years of the present century, on the anniversary of American Independence, a conspicuous feature of the parade was a carriage, contain-ing the survivors of this midnight expedition, in 1772. They were Colonel Ephraim Bowen, Captain Benjamin Page, Colonel John Mawney, and Captain Turpin Smith, and the old banner on which was emblazoned the names of these survivors of that large party of tavern conspirators is yet preserved among the relics in the possession of the Rhode Island Historical Society. The shot fired at Namquit reverberated around the world three years before the minute men of Massachusetts fired upon the redcoats at Concord and Lexing-ton.

During the siege of Boston, in 1775, just outside the line of intrenchments which stretched across the head of Boston Neck, there was located on the road leading into Boston town the famous "St. George" tavern. It was an ad-vance post of the Continental army, and less than a quarter of a mile beyond it were the advanced works of the British army. Many years before the war it had been opened, and widely popular was the landlord who presided over it. In 1721, during the small pox epidemic in Boston, the General Court held its sessions here; the Probate Court for Suffolk county, too, dispatched the busi-ness brought before it for consideration at this time within its walls. The grounds about the house are said to have been beautifully laid out, and a magnificent orchard comprised a part of the tavern estate. The "St. George" tavern occupied an unfortunate position during the siege, for it was on disputed territory and directly in the line of fire of the two contending forces. Its advanced position made it a desirable spot from which to reconnoiter the enemy, and it was well protected by a force of Continentals.

On the fifth of July General Washington and General Lee visited the Roxbury camps, inspected the works thrown up, and continued out to the "St. George," from the grounds of which Washington got his first view of the British advance after taking command of the army.

For weeks the enemy had endeavored to obtain control of this post at the tavern. In the early morning of the twenty-sixth of June a party of British troops advanced down the Neck, and had it not been for the vigilance of the sentinel, would doubtless have captured the guard and destroyed the tavern, but the force turned out quickly, repulsed the attacking party, and they retreated within the British lines. During the next four weeks there were frequent attacks and bombardments, and nearly every farmhouse on the Neck was destroyed. On the fourteenth of July, a Connecticut soldier, says General Heath "was killed in the street in front of the George Tavern. The shot entered his body, drove it some distance, and lodged in him, in a remarkable manner." "On the thirty-first," continues General Heath, in his memoirs, "A little before one o'clock A. M., a British floating battery came up the river, within three hundred yards of Sewall's Point, and fired a number of shot at the American works, on both sides of the river. At the same time the British, on Boston Neck, falling towards Roxbury, drove in the American sentinels, set fire to the George tavern, and returned to their works." Thus went up in flames this famous hostelry.

Some years after peace had been restored, about 1788, another house was erected on the site of the "George," and opened for the entertainment of travellers. It was maintained by a woman named Sally Barton, who provided the novel attraction of bull-baiting for the amusement and edification of her guests. Such performances do not appear to have been uncommon in Massachusetts, for in the *Essex Register* for June, 1809, there may be found this advertisement:

"SPORTSMEN, ATTEND.

The gentlemen **Sportsmen** of this town and its vicinity are informed that a Grand Combat will take place between the URUS ZEBU, and Spanish BULL, on the 4th of July, if fair weather, if not, the next fair day, at the. HALF-WAY HOUSE on the Salem Turnpike. There will also be exposed at the Circus, other Animals,' which, for courage, strength and sagacity, are inferior to none. No danger need be apprehended during the performance, as the Circus is very Convenient.

Doors opened at 3, performance to begin at 4. Tickets 50 cents.

After the performance there will be a good FOX CHASE on the marshes near the Circus, to start precisely at 6 o'clock."

The "Blue Anchor" tavern stood on the old Boston road, a short distance west of the Saugus river. During the Revolution it was kept by Jacob Newhall, a staunch old patriot, who, with a desire to keep up with the times, took down his old sign, and substituted a rising sun, emblematical of the new republic. At the outbreak of hostilities, and the call for troops to assemble around Boston, landlord Newhall made provision to care for the men whom he knew would throng the road by his tavern, on the way to join the grand army, and in order "to provide for such emergencies he kept on hand fatted oxen, from which a sufficient number might be promptly slaughtered." On the morning of the seventeenth of June, 1775, his house was filled with minute men, who had hurriedly armed and equipped themselves, and had set out from their homes in various parts of the colony.

Tired and hungry, they arrived one by one, until a large number were there assembled. He fed them all bounteously, which good treatment so pleased them that the object of their mission in these parts was somewhat lost sight of, and they lounged about the tavern and its cool shades, little thinking of the great need there was of their services at the front. At last the patriotic old landlord could stand it no longer, he admonished them of their duty, and hurried them off where their presence was more necessary than lounging about the tavern.

Alden's tavern at Lebanon, Connecticut, was the scene of that ludicrous encounter with the captive British General Prescott.

After his capture at his headquarters on the island of Rhode Island by General Barton, Prescott was taken to David Arnold's tavern in Warwick, R. I., where he passed the night securely guarded, for he was too important a prisoner to lose sight of. In the morning, he was escorted to Providence, and there turned over, a prisoner of war, to General Spencer. In due time he was sent to New York for exchange. On his journey there the way led through Connecticut and the town of Lebanon, where the party stopped at Alden's tavern to dine. It happened on this occasion that "the landlady brought on the table a dish of succotash (boiled corn and beans). The general, unaccustomed to such kind of food, with much warmth exclaimed, 'What! do you treat us with the food of hogs?' and taking the dish from the table, emptied the contents over the floor. The landlord being informed of this, soon entered with his horsewhip, and gave the general a severe chastisement. After the general was exchanged, and he resumed his command on the island, the inhabitants of Nantucket deputed Dr. Gilston to negotiate some concerns with General Prescott, in behalf of the town. Prescott treated the doctor very cavalierly, and gave as the cause, that the doctor looked so like that d---d landlord who horsewhipped him in Connecticut, that he could not treat him with civility." Prescott was a little, peevish old man, imperious and arbitrary, and the chastisement which he was forced to receive at the hands of mine host Alden was more humiliating to him than his capture. There was a tavern in the town of Bennington, Vt., which was the headquarters for the leading patriots in that section during the war. It bore the euphonious name of the "Catamount" tavern. It was the meeting place of the Council of Safety which included such men as bold Ethan Allen, Chittenden, Stark, Robinson, Warner and other prominent patriots in Vermont. It was the headquarters for that brave band of Green Mountain Boys whose scouts, skilled in woodcraft, first learned of the plan formulated by Burgoyne to attack Bennington and deprive the American Army of its stores. One of the rooms in this hostelry was designated as the "council room," and here these brave men laid their plans and drank good New England rum. The old tavern account book bearing the unbalanced "score" charged against Ethan Allen is yet preserved. Allen was a tower of strength to the cause of liberty; a blunt, honest man of the highest integrity. In religion it is said "he was a free thinker, and passed for an infidel," and this it was that prompted the Rev. Dr. Ezra Stiles to write in the margin of his almanack for the year 1789, against the date February 13, "General Ethan Allen of Vermont died and went to Hell this day." The "Catamount" tavern was destroyed in 1871. Another noted hostelry in Vermont was Coffin's tavern, "situated on the north part of Cavendish, on the old military road, cut out, in the French wars, by the energetic General Amherst, with a regiment of New Hampshire Boys, and extending from Number Four, as Charlestown on the Connecticut was then called, to the fortresses on Lake Champlain." It was presided over by Captain John Coffin, and was the rendezvous for the scouting parties sent out by the Council of Safety in Vermont, and whose services were of so much consequence to the success of the American army at Bennington.

"Pitt's Head" and the "White Horse" were two famous taverns in Newport, and previous to the occupancy of that flourishing seaport by the British army, these two houses were the recruiting stations for that town. Edward Cole was the recruiting officer at the former, while Archibald McKendrick enlisted soldiers for the Continental army at the "White Horse," still standing on Marlborough street.

When the British army took possession of Newport the taverns were the common drinking places of the soldiery. At the "Marquis of Granby" a number of Hessian officers were quartered. Among the servants at the "Marquis" was a young German girl, Gertrude Hegel, a maid-of-all-work. She rapidly picked up the English language, and with her knowledge of German she proved to be a most valuable ally to the loyal farmers on the island who frequented the tavern on market days. Through her many of the points desired by General Spencer for his proposed expedition against the enemy in 1777 were obtained, and had it not been for other causes which interfered, the expedition planned at that time might have proved a more creditable affair than it subsequently turned out.

At Henry Bowen's tavern the Barrington infantry company and artillery company were recruited, and the landlord was the recruiting officer for the town.

The great number of soldiers which Barrington furnished for the army, compared with the population of the town, during the war, testifies to the energetic work of this estimable and picturesque tavern keeper.

The "Green Dragon" tavern in Union street, Boston, has been called the headquarters of the Revolution, for it was another meeting place of the ante-revolutionary patriots, and later was used as a hospital. Of the meetings held here and the schemes concocted, Paul Revere says: "In the fall of 1774 and winter of 1775 I was one of upwards of thirty, chiefly mechanics, who formed ourselves into a committee for the purpose of watching the movements of the British soldiers, and gaining every intelligence of the movements of the Tories. We held our meetings at the Green Dragon tavern. This committee were astonished to find all their secrets known to General Gage, although every time they met every member swore not to reveal any of their transactions, except to Hancock, Adams, Warren, Otis, Church, and one or two more." One of those entrusted with these secrets proved a traitor, for Church was afterwards arrested for treason. How well Revere watched the movements of the British soldiers has been told by the landlord of the "Wayside inn."

The "Black Horse" tavern was between Salem and Hanover streets in Boston, and is said to have been noted as a place of refuge and concealment "for deserters from the British army."

On the occasion of the victory of Stark, at Bennington, there was a grand celebration at the "Bunch of Grapes," in Boston. Early in the evening there began to arrive great numbers of the principal men in the town, as well as strangers, who happened to be "within the gates of the city" at this time. "In the street were two brass fieldpieces, with a detachment of Colonel Craft's regiment." On the balcony of the town house all of the drummers and fifers in one of the regiments then in the town were posted. At a given signal the artillery commenced a salute of thirteen guns. After this the enthusiastic party assembled in the house, drank a series of toasts, following every one of which there was a salute of three guns and a shower of rockets. "About nine o'clock two barrels of grog were brought out into the street for the people that had collected there. It was all conducted with the greatest propriety, and by ten o'clock every man was at his home."

This popular hostelry was situated on what is now State street. Not far away, on the corner of Exchange and State streets, was the "Royal Exchange" tavern, near which occurred the Boston massacre. Many of the British officers had their quarters at this tavern. This deplorable affair was started by the sentinel whose post was in front of the Royal Custom House, directly opposite the tavern.

As in time of peace the town and county courts were held at the taverns, so in war times courts martial were held there, too. It was the custom for the Provost Marshal to provide suitable quarters in which to hold these courts, and having due regard for the comfort of his fellow officers in the disagreeable duty which they were obliged to perform, he provided them with accommodations at the taverns, whenever it was possible to do so, that there might be some cheer about this duty after all.

The orderly book of Colonel Henry Sherburne's Regiment contains many references to such proceedings, the orders usually reading:

"A court martial to set tomorrow 9 o'clock at Mr. Pierces' Innholder at Bristol to try such prisoners as may be brought before them."

For many months this regiment was encamped in Rhode Island, on the east side of Narragansett bay, at the town of Warren. There is evidence that there were sundry incursions upon the farmers' stock near the encampment, for the proceedings of the court martial thus ordered show the following:

"Bristol Jany 9, 1779.

"The Gen Court martial which sat yesterday at Pierces Tavern, is ordered again to convene this day at half an hour past 10 o'clock Forenoon.

"At a Gen Court martial held at Bristol Jany 8 whereof Major Bradford is president was Try'd Sergt Amos Avery & Corp John Paine of Col Sherburne's Regt for Stealing Sheep from the Public & Inhabitants of Bristol. The prisoners being brought before the court plead not guilty. The court after considering the evidence are of opinion that they are guilty and sentance them to be reduced to the ranks & Receive fifty lashes each on their naked Backs and that the value of the Sheep be stop'd from their pay.

"The above sentences are approved & the Prisoners to be punished this afternoon at Retreat beating & their Epeuletts taken from their shoulders.

"Also Tryd by the same Court Wm Grant Ezekiel Chace Eben B. Dickey & Wm Gilbart all Soldiers in Col. Sherburnes Regt for Stealing Sheep from the Public and Inhabitants of Bristol. To which charges they all Plead Guilty. The Court sentence Grant to receive Sixty Lashes on his naked back. Chace to Receive Sixty Lashes on his naked back Likewise. Eben B. Dickey to Receive the same number. But in consequence of the Recommendation of the Court in favor of Dicks incapacity to Withstand the allurements of the Designing he is pardoned Gilbart who's Crime appearing to the Court more aggravated Do Sentance him to Receive one Hundred Lashes on his naked back. And further adjude that Gilbart Chace & Dickey be put under stoppages to the value of one sheep and further that stoppages be made from the pay of Chace Dickey & Gilbart to the value of two sheep it appearing to the Court that Grant was not Present at the Last Theift.

"The above sentences are approved & the prisoners ordered to Receive their Punishment this evening at Retreat Beating and join their Regiment."

Nearly every one of the country taverns throughout the colonies bore some part in the Revolutionary struggle. Its importance in the community naturally made it the rendezvous for the townspeople; within it the patriots of '76 bade their last farewell to friends and neighbors before joining the army; around the board in the dining room the town authorities made provisions for supplying the army in the field and the distressed families of those who were fighting for liberty or had fallen in freedom's cause. Here was received the first news of victory or defeat, and when peace threw her mantle over the contending forces, the walls of the old taverns rang with the shouts of victory, and the returning victors were feted and feasted in the same familiar room wherein they had subscribed to their oaths of enlistment, and where had been laid the plans for the building of a new nation.

Chapter Eight - The Tavern and the Stage Coach

About the middle of the eighteenth century public stage coaches began to run regularly between Boston and other towns in the New England colonies. Boston was the coaching center. Drake, in his *"Landmarks of Boston"* says that the first line of coaches was between Boston and Portsmouth, N. H., and was conducted by Bartholomew Staver. The station of the "Portsmouth Flying Stage Coach" was at the "Lighthouse" tavern, where passengers were booked for the trip. The coach then in use held six inside passengers, and the fare between the two points was "thirteen and six, sterling."

The advantages which these "creaky, mud-covered old caravans" offered for getting from place to place caused many persons to embark in the stage coach business, and ere the close of the century regular lines of Flying stage coaches, mail stages and light "Waggons" were in operation throughout the settled portion of New England. The tavern in those days was to these lines what the depot is to the modern railway systems. Distances were always reckoned from tavern to tavern, the town in which the house was located being merely noted for convenience. The early editions of various almanacks contain these old stage routes, with the various tavern stops, against which will be found the distance between each in miles. Thus, in the *"New England Almanack or Lady's and Gentlemen' s Diary"* for the year 1765, the "Road to Hartford, through Killingly, Pomfret, &c.. From Providence Court House, on the South Road, over the Great Bridge," wound snake-like over hill and dale, through thick woods and meadow land to Jonathan Olney's tavern in Johnston, two miles; then to Joseph Fenner's tavern, one mile farther. From Providence there was another route to the main road, leading to Hartford, which lay by the "North road over the Mill Bridge from Providence Court House" to Ephraim Pearce's tavern in Johnston, where the north and the south roads met. The distance by the north road was one mile and a half more. From the "parting of the roads" the route onward is thus scheduled (see list, next page.)

The first name being the town, the latter that of the tavern keeper, while the figures indicate the distance between each in miles. Many pages of these old almanacks are devoted to this subject. And it was valuable information too, for it was to the people of those early days what the railroad "folder" and time table is to the modern traveller. The almanack maker realized the importance of this part of his publication, and he gave notice to the tavern keeper from year to year by publishing such notices as this, which is taken from Nathaniel Ames almanack for the year 1763:

"☞ It happens every year that some Tavern Keepers in one or other of the Governments give up their License, and others are substituted in their Room:

It is therefore requested for the Benefit of Travellers as well as their inn, that such new Licensed Persons would send a Letter Free of Charge to the Author living at DEDHAM, that it may be inserted in the following years. — They must be particular in expressing the number of miles they are from the stages before & after them."

And again he notes:

"If any good House of Entertainment is omitted, or any inserted that do not keep a Tavern; also if there are any Errors in the Distances of the Stages, it is desired that those who live at or near the Places where the mistakes are, would send a letter to *Richard & Samuel Draper,* Printers in *Boston,* free of charge, and they shall be rectified."

" From Pearce's to	Eddy's	$\frac{1}{4}$
A. Belknap's in	Johnston	$1\frac{1}{2}$
To Smithfield,	Foster's	3
Ditto	Hopkins	1
Gloucester	Wilmarth's	6
Ditto	Smith's	3
Ditto	Barrett	4
Killingsly	Learned	2
Ditto	Falshaw	2
Over the Bridge	Grosvenor	$4\frac{1}{2}$
Ditto	Sessions	4
Ashford	Sumner	2
Ditto	Wales	4
Ditto	Clarke	$2\frac{1}{2}$
Ditto	Fay	$2\frac{1}{2}$
Mansfield	Waterman	4
Coventry	Kimball	8
E. Hartford	Pelkins	7
Ditto	Bidwell	9
Hartford	Flagg or Bull	2 "

The middle road from Boston to Hartford and New Haven lay through Medfield, where the first change of horses was made, twenty-five miles out from Boston. The regular stop was at Clarke's tavern. Long before the coach reached the village the sound of the coach bugle gave warning to the hostlers that it was approaching and to get ready the hitch. Eleven miles out of Boston the coach had made its stop at the Ames Tavern, at Dedham, then on to Colburn's in the same town, then on again to Medfield, where it had drawn up at the Clarke tavern, where the first stop of any consequence was made. From there the way led through Medway, Bellingham, Milford, Uxbridge, Douglas, Thompson, Pomfret, Ashford, Wilmington, Mansfield, Coventry, East Hartford, and finally drew up at Bull's tavern, in Hartford.

The evening of the arrival of the coach was a lively one at the tavern. Eager townsmen, hoping for information from distant towns, would drop in one by one, mingle with the day's arrivals around the fire in the great room, and listen with attentive ears to the news that they related. Packages containing some long looked for article or some little memento from distant friends were sometimes sent by the passengers to brighten for days and even weeks afterward, the hearts of the recipients. Around the comfortable fire the assembled company would discuss all manner of subjects; politics, however, was the main subject. In this way the people obtained the views and opinions of those in the surrounding governments, and which influenced them in their actions at home.

Toddy, flip and other drinks were generously passed around, until tired and worn out with the day's trip, and the long talks, the new arrivals gradually withdrew from the circle and retired to their rooms.

The tavern was the "booking" place for the trip. Here the prospective traveller would repair and write in the book which the stage line provided, his name and the place where the stage was to call for him. Perhaps he might stop at the tavern that night, in order to be on hand promptly when the stage started. The time taken in the journey can be understood by the following notice in the *"New England Town and County Almanack"* for 1769: "The Norwich coach comes once a week from Mr. Azariah Lathrop's, in Norwich, to Dr. Samuel Carew's, on the west side of the Great Bridge, in Providence, where travellers will meet with the best entertainment. The stage performed in a day." At the same time it was also announced: "The Providence coaches kept by Mr. Thomas Sabin and Knight Dexter, Esq., go twice a week from Providence to Boston, performing their respective stages in a day." For more than twenty years travel between these towns was limited to three trips each week, but about 1793 Israel Hatch put on a "line of stages," and issued the following notice to the travelling public:

"Boston and Providence Stages. Israel Hatch

Most respectfully informs the publick that his line of Stages will run every day in the week, excepting Sundays. His Coach leaves *Boston* at 5 o'clock, and arrives at *Providence* by 2 P. M. The Stages from *Providence* start at the same early hour, and arrive at *Boston* by 2 o'clock. Twenty-four excellent horses, six good coaches, and as many experienced drivers are always provided. The horses will be regularly changed at the half-way house, in Walpole. Passengers may be accommodated with places at the sign of the Grand Turk, No. 25 Newbury street, Boston; at Mrs. Catharine Gray's, State street; at Col. Colman's, *State Street*; and in Providence, at Mrs. Rice's, the sign of the Golden Ball; or at Mr. Coggeshall's, the sign of the Coach and Horses.

☞ *Price from Providence to Boston, or from Boston to Providence, is only* One Dollar, *which is one half the customary price, and is cheaper than any other stage*, —

Twenty pounds of baggage is allowed; and every 100 wt. rated at 6s.

Books will be kept at each of the abovementioned places, for the insertion of the names of Passengers.

*** He cannot but hope for the encouragement of the public. He is sincerely thankful for past favours; and anticipates a continuance of them. He is also determined, at the expiration of the present contract for conveying the Mail from Providence to Boston to carry it gratis; which will undoubtedly prevent any further underbiddings of the envious.

Boston, June 15, 1793."

At the same time Thomas Beals, operating a rival line of Mail Stage Carriages, issued his advertisement:

"BOSTON AND PROVIDENCE STAGE.

The subscriber informs his friends and the Publick, that he for the more rapid conveyance of the Mail Stage Carriage, genteel, and easy, has good horses, and experienced, careful drivers.

They will start from *Boston and Providence*, and continue to run three times each week, until the first of November. — Will leave *Boston* every Monday, Wednesday, and Friday at 5 o'clock A.M., and arrive at Providence the same days at 2 o'clock P.M. They will leave *Providence* Tuesdays, Thursdays, and Saturdays at 5 o'clock A.M., and arrive at Boston the same days at 2 o'clock P.M.

The Price for each passenger, will be *Nine shillings* only, and less, if any other person will carry them for that sum. Twenty pounds of baggage gratis.

Also a good new Philadelphia-built light Waggon, to go the other days in the week, if wanted — and as the proprietor has been at such great expense to erect the Line, he hopes his exertions will give satisfaction, and receive the public patronage.

Ladies and Gentlemen, who wish to take passage in this Stage, will please to apply for seats, at the house of the Subscriber in Dock Square, at Col. Colman's, or Mrs. Gray's, State street, as the Stage will set out from each of those places; books are there kept for entering passenger's name. The Stage will start from Coggeshall's Tavern in *Providence,* formerly kept by Knight Dexter, Esq.

THOMAS BEALS.

Boston, June 15, 1793."

The "Stable and Horses" was at this time the news center of the town, for the passengers here "set down" brought from time to time the happenings in many sections of New England. Landlord Dexter of this famous caravansary had been a progressive man, and called attention to the excellence and advantages of his establishment by this advertisement, which he caused to be printed in the *Providence Gazette*:

"Food for the Hungry, Drink for the
Thirsty and a home for the
Weary Traveler.
Knight Dexter,

Begs leave to inform the public in general, and all his old friends and customers in particular. That he has again opened a House of Entertainment, at that noted place the sign of the Stable and Horses, opposite Messieurs Joseph and William Russels in the main street, where he formerly devoted his time to procure refreshments. Ease and Entertainment for the traveler and man of business.

He has laid in the very best of Provisions, Liquors &c and those persons who favor him with their custom may depend on the best treatment."

The arrival of the stage coach at one of these taverns was the weekly, semi-weekly or tri-weekly event of the town.

The rumble and rattle of the lumbering old vehicle over the rough country roads, gave warning of its coming long before it came in sight. If the tavern was a "change station," where a fresh team of horses was hitched, then the sound of the bugle or horn would be heard echoing through the woods or reverberating over the hills. At these sounds of warning the villagers, who always made it a point to be on hand when the coach arrived, began to assemble about the tavern yard.

The loungers in the bar room slowly roused themselves from their reverie, shook themselves together, and shuffled across the sanded floor to the doorway, where the landlord, full of smiles and graces, stood waiting to welcome the guests. With a snapping of whip and loud "whoas!" from the red-faced driver, the coach swung into the driveway to the tavern, and hauled up before its door. Then all was bustle and excitement. The tired, road-stained passengers were let out of the vat shaped box, stretched their limbs, and, with a satisfied look that they had escaped disaster, entered the tavern, and were soon besieged by all of those who had congregated, for news from the outer world. The driver of the coach at such times was a most important individual. He had news for everybody and of every kind. Many a sly bit of scandal had been picked up by him while he had waited for dinner or for the horses to be changed. He knew every one that had left the coach during the trip and whither they went. He had left a message at the Thurber homestead that Captain Thurber's ship had arrived at Boston just before he had started, direct from Surinam, and would himself be down on the next coach if he could arrange matters regarding the cargo.

The new minister had arrived, and was left at Deacon Parks, where a number of the people were gathered to receive him. There had been an earthquake at Lisbon. A cassowary was on exhibition at a tavern on the road. There was much snow to the northward, or the crops were all blasted with the drought at the southward. He had news of all kinds which was as welcome to the eager listeners as was the fiery liquids which he took at the bar to wash away the dust that had accumulated during the last few miles of the trip. Stage drivers were selected with great ca-re; they were men of ability, prudence and experience. On the driver of the coach depended the safety of the outfit and the human freight which it contained.

Captain Ezra Lunt of Newburyport, who kept the tavern at that place, and led the singing in the meeting house on Sundays, before he took charge of the tavern, drove the first four-horse coach line between Newburyport and Boston, and was a man of high character and great influence in this town.

Joseph Wyman, who run the stage between Boston and Medford, had the remarkable record of driving for thirty-four years continuously, twice a day, without an accident of any kind. His stage left Medford at eight o'clock in the morning, and started from Wild's tavern in Elm street, Boston, at four o'clock in the afternoon. This coach carried ten passengers. The number of passengers which a coach usually carried depended somewhat on the character of the trip. If it was a mail coach it was limited to six passengers, otherwise eight or ten were carried. The length of the trip sometimes regulated this. On the long stages not more than six passengers could be comfortably carried, while on the shorter ones more.

The price, too, varied, and for travelling by the mail coaches a greater sum was charged than by the slow coaches. Four horses were commonly used, except in the spring time and winter. The roads in those early days were not of a high order. Little money and little labor was expended upon them, for it was not until the days of the Turnpike Companies that the highways were kept in any kind of repair. In the spring time the mud was anywhere from twelve to eighteen inches deep, and in the lowlands ever deeper, while in the winter season the drifting snow made it almost impossible to put the coach through at all. At these seasons six horses were always hitched to the coach.

The condition of the roads at the period of the Revolutionary war is shown by the statement of one who made a trip from Providence to Pomfret, for he says: "In May, 1776, I went to Pomfret, thirty-six miles in a chaise; the road was so stony and rough, that I could not ride out of a slow walk, but very little of the way; I was near two days in going, such was the general state of our roads at that time."

The coaches themselves have been likened to "diving bells," "distiller's vats," "violincello cases hung equally balanced between front and back springs," and having a motion "like a ship rocking or beating against a heavy sea; straining all her timbers with a low moaning sound as she drives over the contending waves."

Coaching in early New England was not altogether unlike that in old England in the seventeenth century.

A pessimistic stage coach traveller in England has left the following synopsis of his adventures in the stage coach. It illustrates some of the joys and sorrows of coaching in New England in the early days of the road, as well as it does the experiences in old England's coaches. It is found in Tristam's entertaining story of "*Coaching Days and Coaching Ways.*"

Inside — Crammed full of passengers — three fat, fusty old men — a young mother and sick child — a cross old maid — a poll parrot — a bag of red herrings — double barrelled gun (which you are afraid is loaded)— and a snarling lap dog in addition to yourself — Awake out of a sound nap with the cramp in one leg and the other in a lady's band box — pay the damage (four or five shillings) for gallantry's sake — getting out in the dark at the half-way house, in the hurry stepping into the return coach and finding yourself next morning at the very spot you had started from the evening before — not a breath of air — asthmatic old woman and child with the measles — window closed in consequence — unpleasant smell — shoes filled with warm water — look up and find its the child — obliged to bear it — no appeal — shut your eyes and scold the dog — pretend sleep and pinch the child — mistake — pinch the dog and get bit, — Execrate the child in return — black looks — no gentleman — pay the coachman and drop a piece of gold in the straw — not to be found — fell through a crevice — coachman says 'He'll find it!' — can't — get out yourself — gone — picked up by the ostler — no time for blowing up — coach off for next stage — lose your money — get in — lose your seat — stuck in the middle — get laughed at — lose your temper — turn sulky — and turned over in a horse pond."

"Outside, — your eye cut out by the lash of a clumsy Coachman's whip — hat blown off into a pond by a sudden gust of wind — seated between two apprehended murderers and a noted sheep stealer in irons — who are being conveyed to gaol — a drunken fellow half asleep falls off the Coach — and in attempting to save himself drags you along with him into the mud — musical guard, and driver horn mad — turned over — one leg under a bale of cotton — the other under the Coach — hands in breeches pockets — head in hamper of wine — lots of broken bottles versus broken heads — cut and run — send for surgeon — wounds dressed — lotion and lint four dollars— take post chaise — get home — lay down — and laid up."

The stable adjoining the tavern was an important adjunct to the house. Besides the horses which were used on the coaches the landlord had a few extra beasts for the use of travellers and other patrons of his establishment. These were let for many purposes and the tavern account books show the extent to which this department of the inn was patronized. Here was put up the traveller's horse, and here the townsmen could hire a horse or horse and vehicle at the general price of three pence a mile. For odd jobs the price was regulated according to the nature of the service performed, as the following:

> "To my horse to grind bark 2 or 3 hours 8s."
> "To my horse to harro 1½ acres of corn 1od."
> "To my horse and cart to go to John Jacobs
>   for lime 1s 4d"
> "To my bay horse & cart to Cart 1 Load of
>   Onions 9s."
> "To my horse & cart to cart stalks 6s."
> "To my bay horse and cart to cart yr flax
>   2s 6d."
> "To my horse to ride to meeting o ʋ 8."

There is a suggestion of discrimination in the conduct of the stable of one tavernkeeper in the charge which he makes upon his book, for under the date October 10, 1775, there is entered:

"Lieut. James Smith Dr

For keeping your horse 6 days after the best manner 3s."

Perhaps in the management of the stable there were several "manners" of keeping horses, one of which was the "best manner," but a careful examination of the account books fails to disclose what the other "manners" were and their prices.

On Henry Bowen's Barrington tavern account book there may be found frequent charges for the use of his carts and horses. Among these is a most curious entry. From this it appears that Hezekiah Kinnicut had occasion to attend a funeral of his brother's child, and like most of his neighbors on such occasions, he resorted to Bowen's for a conveyance. On August 18, 1777, Henry Bowen wrote upon his book this charge:

"Hezekiah Kinnicut, Dr.

To nay Slay over to the Funeral of ye Brother Shubael's child, and almost wore out the runners, 6s."

If this entry is of the same date as the funeral of Shubael's child, a "slay" would seem to be a peculiar conveyance for midsummer, and there seems to be some reason in assuming it to be so, for he "almost wore out the runners." The wear on the horse does not appear to have been considered.

When an outfit was procured for a trip to a neighboring town the charge was three pence a mile, and the entries for such read as follows:

> "To my horse to ride to Seaconet,
> 24 miles, at 3d, 6s."
> "To my hors and cart to go to
> Josiah Kent of Rehoboth, 10d."

Careful accounts were kept of the expenses of the stable; "shooing," horse "steeling two before," and other charges were carefully noted.

Along in the month of December the coaches run less regularly. The chill winter winds discouraged travel, except in cases of emergency. Snow, too, filled the roadways, and often blocked them for weeks. There are numerous instances of heavy storms of snow overtaking the coach on the trip, and drifting so badly that all progress is impeded. The plunging of the "leaders" tangled the harness, broke the pole, and overturned the coach; then there was trouble. The last tavern that the coach had passed is five miles back in the face of a drifting snow storm; the next one beyond is about the same distance, with the storm increasing; it is growing dark, too, and the air is biting cold. Six shivering, furiously mad individuals stand looking at the overturned coach and uttering strange oaths. To remain a great while in such a place means to freeze. The nearest house or shelter is the tavern, distant either way five miles. The driver climbs up on to the box of the coach and brings forth the necessary appliances for starting a light. He orders the shivering passengers to assist in procuring wood enough to start a fire and keep it burning, while he mounts one of the horses and braves the storm for help.

At the tavern beyond, the wind whistles down the chimney, now and then blowing the smoke out into the great room where the men folks of the house are assembled in the growing darkness.

"There'll be no coach to-night. Akerman never 'd start from the 'Buck' with this storm in the air," says mine host, as he walks to the window and gazes upon the white landscape and flying snowflakes.

"No," replies the hostler, who has sought the comfortable warmth of the tap room, "it's driften bad and he'd never get through with that pair of 'wheelers.'"

"They'll put up at the 'Buck' to-night," chimes in the hostess. "It's just our luck, Daniel," she adds, turning to the landlord, "the coach never gets further than Knox's when there's a storm, and there they'll stay for two or three days, and after you've helped 'break the roads,' and they 're again on the road they'll go ridin' by here without so much as a smile on their face or taking a drop with us."

"Hark! what's that?" suddenly shouts the hostler, and all rush to the window. "Some one on horseback, shouting and waving his hands like mad." "Well, I vum, its Akerman," replies the landlord, and he and the hostler grab their hats and run into the yard to meet the horseman who has now come into the driveway.

"What's up, Akerman?"

"Coach on its side and six of 'em up there about five miles freezing in the woods; you'll have to put a fresh pair in the pung, and go up and get 'em."

There is no need of any further discussion. The biting wind and the whirling flakes stimulate the stable hands to quick work, and before Akerman has fully thawed himself out at the fire place, two hostlers, well bundled up with robes and blankets, are on the way to the rescue, yelling and snapping the whip over two powerful grays, who are throwing the dry snow in great clouds right and left as they plunge down the road.

Mistress, in anticipation of seven hungry persons coming in upon her, is busily engaged, with a satisfied look on her face, for the "Buck" will not have the guests this time. Akerman, sufficiently thawed out to enjoy a hot toddy, sits contentedly by the fireside and explains the disaster to the landlord, and thus the time drags on until well along into the evening, when the pung, with its six half frozen travellers and the team of the overturned coach, arrive at the inn. And what a cheerful place it is after these hours of exposure to a bitter winter storm, and how well the hot cakes, coffee and bacon harmonized with their faint stomachs, and how right to the spot does the hot toddy find its way, and how well did the old time tavern keeper and his good wife know how to soften the hearts of such travellers, when they came to the inn with empty stomachs, fussing and swearing over their misfortunes.

The supper being over, the weather bound passengers repair to the great room, light their pipes, and now so comfortably settled, with their hunger appeased, they regard their adventure more as a joke, and seem contented to remain a week; and such proves to be the result, for after two days of driving snow, the roads are left in such condition that here they must remain snowed up.

Snow storms were not the only disturbing element in coaching, for on the ninth of October, 1804, during a violent gale of wind, a stage coach, in crossing the West Boston bridge, was blown over and several of its passengers severely injured. With the passing of the stage coach the tavern, too, soon followed. It had served its purpose; a change had come and it quietly closed its doors. The tavern sign is relegated to the museum collections and the landlord and lady, whose cheerful smiles greeted the traveller, when, tired, stained and hungry, he climbed from the box, now sleep side by side in the little God's acre on the Post Road.

Along the country roads and on the city's busy streets many of these weather-beaten old structures, once the scene of so much life and activity, still serve to recall memories of departed days. But all else is changed. There is no crowd of curious townsmen hanging about the doors, eager to catch a glimpse of the coaching book and scan the names of the coming and parting guests. The echoes of the coach horn, which awakened so much excitement and anticipation, have faded away. The great room wherein the townsmen and travellers met and discussed the great questions of public concern, and the good qualities of New England rum, is deserted, for...

"Long ago at the end of its route,
The stage pulled up and the folks stepped out.
They have all passed under the tavern door,
The youth and his bride and the gray threescore.
Their eyes were weary with dust and gleam.
The day had gone like an empty dream.
Soft may they slumber, and trouble no more
For their eager journey, its jolt and roar,
On the old road over the mountain!"

The New England tavern as an institution has vanished, but its importance as an educational factor in the life of New England will always remain.

www.ingramcontent.com/pod-product-compliance
Lightning Source LLC
Chambersburg PA
CBHW051840040426
42447CB00006B/625